The Psychology of Abusive Relationships

How to recognize the signs of a toxic relationship, unmask a narcissistic personality and regain control of your life!

Melany Bennet

TABLE OF CONTENT

Chapter one:

INTRODUCTION

Tears streamed down her face as she glanced down at her brittle wrists engraved with scathing marks that would soon turn from crimson red to a dullish blue at the same time the sun rose. The fear of what he might do next outweighed her need to seek help from the authorities. 911, the numbers she'd memorized since she was five years old, felt like anchors pulling at her chest. She knew what she had to do. The elephant in the room was when. Amid all the turbulence, she couldn't help but blame herself for all that transpired.

Unfortunately, this situation is the harsh reality for millions of individuals across the globe. It is estimated that nearly 5 million women in the United States alone endure some form of physical abuse from a romantic partner on a yearly basis. Out of those women, roughly 1,300 of them won't make it out alive.

Contrary to popular belief, abuse isn't limited to

physical harm. Nearly 50% of women have experienced some form of emotional abuse from their significant other at least once in their lifetime.

The statistics don't stop there. A recent study found that 1 in 10 men have experienced some form of rape or sexual assault. That statistic is doubled in women, bringing their likelihood of experiencing sexual abuse to 1 in 5.

Furthermore, abuse transcends the confines of romantic relationships. Abuse, in its many forms, take shape in platonic, professional and even familial relationships.

The internet has opened the threshold to a new form of abuse, most commonly referred to as cyberbullying. This digital harassment affects 1 in 4 teenagers and often leads to physical or sexual abuse over time.

With abuse so prevalent in today's society, it begs the answer to one simple question: why? Why do people abuse others? Why do victims remain attached to their abusers; even if they aren't romantically involved? Why aren't there lasting solutions to this epidemic?

This e-book is designed to take a deep dive into the mind of an abuser. We'll begin by identifying common behavioral patterns to help readers develop a deeper understanding of this topic. By doing so, those suffering from an unhealthy dynamic will hopefully have the tools needed to escape the perils of abuse.

What Is Abuse?

Abuse in layman's terms is defined as "a corrupt practice or custom." Interestingly, the terms "practice" and "custom" are synonymous with repetition. This aligns with the concept that abuse, in any fashion, is not singular but rather, repetitive. Victims of abuse are often subjected to multiple offenses in any given period. In some cases, such as with narcissistic or psychological abuse, the victim is unaware that their partner's actions are considered abusive. Because of this, the actual percentage of individuals who have suffered and survived abuse are unknown.

Because repeated behavior is a definitive marker of abuse, it's safe to conclude that those who so freely demonstrate violent and aggressive tendencies either came from or experienced some form of abuse in their formative years. This statement is backed by an analysis written by Follette Polusny, MA, who determined that children exposed to abuse over an extended time grew up to experience severe psychological disorders including aggression. This front-row seat to abuse subconsciously showed vulnerable children how to control, manipulate and hurt others. Their developmental skills are unfortunately warped, causing them to become blissfully unaware of how to solve common problems without resorting to violence, harsh words or control.

A recent study followed the lives of 1,296 children until they turned 29. Out of the selection, 676 came from abusive homes whereas the remaining 520 did not. The concluding results of the study were astounding. Nearly 40% of the participants who experienced some form of childhood abuse were "more likely to have been arrested for a violent crime." The study also found that those same children were more likely to engage in problem behaviors as they grew older.

Now that we've gotten a clear idea of how abuse is defined, let's consider the many faces of abuse and how they can appear in everyday instances.

What Are the Different Forms of Abuse?

According to the World Health Organization, there are four different types of abuse. These forms of mistreatment are most commonly found within domestic and interpersonal relationships. However, some of the same trends are found amongst friends, colleagues and religious leaders. Let's consider each form in its entirety to gain a broader perspective of this behavior choice.

Physical Abuse

According to the National Domestic Violence Hotline, nearly 24 people are beaten every minute. 15% of men and 4% of men in romantic relationships experience injuries due to these violent outbursts.

Physical abuse involves inflicting physical harm on a person or putting them in danger. These actions come in the form of kicking, biting, punching, scratching or shoving. Often, these brazen acts leave victims with nasty bruises and severe injuries.

Physical abuse goes far beyond kicks and punches. Other forms of physical abuse may include denying a person access to medication, withholding food or water or locking someone out of the home for an extended period. Accordingly, putting someone in the line of danger is also be considered physical abuse. This includes purposeful reckless driving or tainting food and water sources.

Sexual Abuse

Sexual abuse is a complex form of mistreatment because it takes advantage of a person in their most vulnerable state. Forcing someone to engage in sexual practices, whether they physically or orally say otherwise, is considered sexual abuse. In the past, researchers considered forced rape as the primary form of sexual abuse. Now, the tentacles of sexual abuse have grown. If someone forces another to engage in sexual acts through coercive statements, guilt trips or threats, they are now engaging in sexual abuse even if the victim doesn't blatantly refuse the offer. This newfound discovery plays into the psyche of a victim and exhibits a toxic form of control. Researchers have found that psychological forms of sexual abuse are just as damaging and traumatic as physical force.

Another lesser known form of sexual abuse is withholding sexual contact as a means of punishment. The abuser always has to feel in control and this sometimes comes before their primal needs. If their victim did something that they deemed reprehensible, they'll reprimand them to make a statement. This dynamic places the victim in a child-like state and robs them of their dignity.

Verbal Abuse

Verbal abusers often exhibit symptoms of narcissistic personality disorder. They use a combination of coercion, psychological manipulation and gas lighting to taunt their victims. Often, victims who suffer verbal abuse have a hard time distinguishing this form of abuse as it appears in subtle ways.

Verbal abuse goes far beyond someone being mean or cranky. Examples that fall under the category of verbal abuse are:

- Attacks on the victim's character;

- Disrespectful comments about their weight or appearance;

- Condescending insults that jab at the victim;

- Putting the victim down in front of others;

- Making "jokes" at the expense of the victim;

- Overtly critical comments.

Verbal abusers leave their victims feeling incapable of happiness to success. Because their comments are critical, the victim often suffers from low self-worth and esteem issues.

Psychological Abuse

Psychological abuse is the perfect storm of verbal and emotional abuse. The main goal of the abuser is to make the victim feel powerless and in need of their approval. This is often done by withholding funds, reprimanding the victim, giving the silent treatment and guilt trips. The victim is left questioning their mental state.

Often, psychological abuse involves making the victim believing that they're the problem. The abuser may make blatant comments like, "Because you're so crazy, I had to lock you out of the home." Or, "If you just stop overreacting, I wouldn't have to yell at you." Instead of rationally discussing issues, the abuser will blame the victim for their actions and engage in a coercive guilt trip that leaves the victim feeling hopeless.

As hurtful as psychological abuse is, it is extremely difficult to measure. Since there are no physical signs of assault, this makes identifying it complicated. Although it's difficult to "prove" from a medical stance, that doesn't make it any less debilitating. Individuals who suffer from psychological abuse may experience difficulty with decision making, self-esteem, and motivation.

Although these are the four main types of abuse recognized on a national level, that doesn't mean there aren't other subdivisions of this epidemic. Neglect, cultural abuse, and religious control are also lesser-known forms of abuse that leave lasting effects.

What Are the Signs of Abuse?

The interesting thing about abusers is that they normally don't start off being violent or aggressive. If they did, nobody in their right mind would want to be around them. Unfortunately, abusers give off a sweet and caring persona. This is what initially attracts the victim and draws them in. As the abuser gets comfortable, the mask comes off and their true intentions are shown.

The vast majority of physical abuse cases begin with verbal or emotional abuse. The abuser may make sly comments here and there to plant the seed of control. As time goes on, their abuse grows more intense; leaving the victim powerless. Although their abuse is deliberate, many abusers don't own up to their actions, even when confronted by their victim. Often, they'll deny the abuse or gaslight their victims to believe it's all in their heads.

Physical abusers will oftentimes deliberately hit their victims in places that are hidden from the public. Because the victim's bruises and scarring go unseen, it's increasingly difficult for them to receive help from an outside source. To gain liberation, the victim must take it upon themselves to contact the authorities for assistance. Sadly, this level of strength can take months, even years, for a victim to attain.

The symptoms of victims suffering from physical or emotional abuse are subjective to each person. How each victim processes their trauma varies. One individual could experience a complete personality shift while the other carries on as if nothing is happening. This is due in part to how the victim views their abuse. If an individual is suffering from emotional or psychological abuse, they may live in denial. Because they don't have physical scarring, they may believe they're being too sensitive. Unfortunately, this mentality is what prevents victims from receiving the help they need.

The concept that abuse goes far beyond the physical is challenging for some people. Besides, the perception of abuse also varies from person to person. For example, if someone was raised by overly critical parents, they may not view their verbally abusive partner as someone toxic. They may brush off direct insults or coercion due to their troubling childhood. Cultural and socioeconomic differences play a vital role in how victims perceive their abuse as well. If a victim comes from a culture that doesn't believe in seeking help from the authorities, the victim is more likely to stay in an unhealthy relationships to abide by their communal norms.

Generational trauma is another contributing factor that inhibits victims from recognizing their abuse and seeking help. Several older individuals were raised with a "pull yourself up by your bootstraps" mentality. This kept them in toxic relationships for an extended period. Despite the progress that researchers and modern psychologists have made to prove the validity of emotional, verbal and psychological abuse, many come from a background where the validity of those behaviors isn't accepted. Therefore, they project those thoughts and instill them in future generations. If a victim happens to come from this type of background, they'll more than likely brush off their abuse and suffer in silence.

Now that we've identified what abuse is, and looked at the different forms and common signs, let's consider a new facet to this discussion: abusive tactics.

The Power and Control Wheel

Within each category lies corresponding behaviors that add to the unfortunate reality of abuse. Each of these tactics all works together to break down the victim and leave them powerless. As we continue, we'll discuss those tactics in further detail to shed light on this complex behavioral pattern. What's interesting about these tactics is that they often overlap, making it extremely difficult for the victim to gain any control.

The National Domestic Violence Hotline developed the Power and Control Wheel in 1984. This tool breaks down the eight tactics that abusers use, ranging from physical to psychological. In many recovery programs, abusers must dissect each piece of this wheel to learn how their behavior fits into each category. Often, these weekly lessons are court-mandated. The only way they can pass the program in its entirety is if they demonstrate a complete understanding of their actions and how it impacted their victims.

The Power and Control Wheel are also used to help victims make sense of their experience. As we'll later cover, those who have suffered from abusive relationships on any level often don't recognize their being abused until years later. Fortunately, with the development of this resource, thousands of men and women across the nation understand their experience on a deeper level. Often, this clarity provides the momentum that pushes them to take that first step towards liberation.

The Tactics That Abusers Use

There are eight ways abusers seek to dominate and control their victims as mentioned in the Power and Control Wheel. Those include:

- Male Privilege;

- Coercion and Threats;

- Intimidation;

- Emotional Abuse;

- Isolation;

- Minimizing, Denying and Blaming;

- Using Children;

- Economic Abuse.

Let's consider each in further detail. It's important to note that while women account for the majority of the abuse statistics, the listed forms of control apply to men as well.

Male Privilege

A 1998 study conducted by Shettima AG entitled "Exploring three layers of exploitation" found that women in Africa are more likely to be controlled and dominated by their male counterparts due to tradition and "socialization patterns." As the growing awareness of equality between the sexes expanded globally, several African women sought to gain their independence. As a result of this craving for power, men "felt threatened and resorted to violence as a form of resistance." This resulted in a severe blow to the male ego thus resulting in increased physical violence on the public level.

This statistic merely scratches the surface of the millions of women across the world who are exposed to abuse as a result of male privilege.

This begs the question, where does male privilege come from and why does it most certainly lead to some form of abuse?

Thomas Keith beautifully explained male privilege in, "Masculinities in Contemporary American Culture: An Intersectional Approach to the Complexities" as "putting systems in place that assure the continued subordination of women in a host of ways and degrees." While not all forms of subordination cross the lines into abuse, it's important to note the similarities between men who exude sexism and the quality of their interpersonal relationships. It isn't far-fetched to assume that if pushed beyond their egotistical threshold, the seeds of abuse would blossom.

The exact age of exposure to male privilege varies from family-to-family and depends heavily on cultural norms. However, it's safe to conclude that young boys are exposed to snippets of male privilege as early as infancy. As they grow older, those seeds of superiority can either grow into full-fledged sexism or fizzle out as a mere fragment of their childhood. Modern research attributes this fork in the road to a few socio-economic factors such as exposure to resources and family dynamics.

Young boys who are exposed to violent, sexist fathers are more likely to demonstrate those views on female partners if this mentality isn't corrected through education and positive reinforcement. Furthermore, boys who are exposed to man-on-woman abuse within the home are more likely to exhibit those same character patterns if they don't receive proper correction. Unfortunately, if the child's economic status is lower, the likelihood that they'll have exposure to forms of correction such as rehabilitation programs or educational resources are slim. Therefore, this creates a never-ending cycle of male dominance over women. This dominance takes on the form of verbal abuse, control, and isolation.

Coercive Control

Coercion is like peer pressure on steroids. It's most commonly defined as "instilling fear or compliance" in someone by making physical and non-physical threats. For example, an emotionally abusive woman may coerce her husband into having sexual relations with her, even if he doesn't want to, by making false accusations about his character or threatening to leave or "out" him with an embarrassing secret. This form of control is often subtle and it usually ends with the abuser getting what they want.

Unfortunately, this off-set of abuse is all too common in romantic and platonic relationships. A recent statistic found that 86% of those in an abusive relationship experience some form of coercive control. That statistic doesn't account for the thousands, possibly millions of individuals suffering in silence or plain ignorance.

Although this form of abuse is non-violent, what makes it so destructive? Mahatma Gandhi once quoted, "One who uses coercion is guilty of deliberate violence. Coercion is inhuman." Words hold value when analyzing the debilitating effects of coercive behavior. At the core lives the dreaded marriage of manipulation and the abuser's selfish agenda. The act of brewing fear within a relationship is cruel and creates a sense of insecurity that's difficult to shake.

Social psychologists sought to test the depth of manipulation through the infamous Milgram experiment. This test unveiled the lengths at which subordinates would go to obey those they deemed powerful. Stanley Milgram created a false scenario consisting of three roles: the participants, the learner and those in authority, also known as, the teachers. The participants and the teachers were in one room while the student was left behind a glass window. The teachers asked each learner a question. For every wrong answer, the participant was instructed by the teacher to deliver an "electric shock" to the learner. Unbeknownst to the participant, the shocks were fake and the learners were actors.

The participant was then instructed by the teachers to raise the voltage of each shock despite seeing the reaction of the learner. The students, being excellent actors, reacted in a way that exhibited great pain and distress. Despite the outcome, the participants continued to listen to those in authority.

It's easy to deem the participants as weak, even cruel for following through with such a heinous act. However, the reality of the test begs to differ. The participants were manipulated by the teachers to obey their actions despite knowing the difference between right and wrong. That short exposure to someone they deemed to hold authority was enough to throw rational decision-making out of the window.

A recent publication explored the connection between coercion and the Milgram experiment. From their research, this gem stood out, "Social coercion may alter mechanisms of voluntary agency, and hence abolish the normal experience of being in control of one's actions."

hese participants had no emotional connection, familial bond or additional reliance on the teacher. Yet, they were coerced into behaving abnormally. Imagine the severity of mental dilapidation that victims experience when they spend an extended amount of time with their abuser. Surely, their level of rational thinking is at an all-time low, making them more susceptible to self-destructive behavior.

Intimidation

Intimidating victims with the hopes of evoking a behavioral change is a popular device used by repeat abusers. Unfortunately, this issue is deeper than the occasional eye roll or raised hand. This severe display of authority ranges from breaking personal belongings, simulating physical harm or flaunting dangerous weapons.

Intimidation can also become physical. However, it usually doesn't involve the victim directly. The abuser may inflict harm on children, pets or strangers to send a message to the victim. This dominant display of power makes the victim fearful of their well-being and pushes them to comply with the demands of the abuser.

Studies have shown that intimidating or "bullying" behavior on an abusive level changes the biology of the brain. This makes the victim more susceptible to developing a mental illness, like anxiety, over time.

The two parts of the brain that are most affected by intimidation tactics are the caudate and putamen. These two areas may not get the same attention as well-known parts like the hippocampus or frontal lobe. However, these two play a vital role in cognitive behavior. Let's zoom in on how the caudate works individually.

The caudate is like the body's internal memory cage. It helps regulate decision making based on memories or experiences. For example, if you had a bad experience at a restaurant years ago, your caudate is responsible for reminding you of that experience with the hopes of swaying your actions.

When a person is abused using intimidation, the caudate, i.e. the bridge between memory and behavior is broken. This could explain why several victims of abuse stay in abusive relationships. As the structure of their brain is altered, they are unable to utilize rational decision making. Researcher Erin Burke Quinlan believes that this drastic change not only sways decision making, but also taints, reward sensitivity, motivation, conditioning, attention, and emotional processing. This means that the victim is more likely to be persuaded by manipulation or toxic control even after they flee the abusive relationship. This could also explain why those who have been abused tend to attract abusers throughout their lives.

The correlation between anxiety and intimidation is strong, especially if this tactic is used within the household. The victim may feel afraid to make a mistake or behave in a way that's displeasing to the abuser out of fear. This creates a tense environment that doesn't support healthy development.

Economic Control

Economic control is one of the leading reasons as to why people stay in abusive relationships even when they know they're being abused. Unfortunately, this form of control is one of the most powerful tactics due to the nature of our society.

Economic control is most commonly found in an abusive relationship between romantic partners. One partner uses intimidation and control to prevent the other from making or spending money. Even if the victim makes their own money, the abuser may take control of where the money goes. By forcing their victim to ask them for money or issuing an "allowance", the abuser is sending a message of codependency. They want their abusers to rely on them for everything to make sure they don't leave. Since the victim has no access to monetary support, they have no choice but to remain in an abusive relationship if they want to get their immediate needs met.

Abusers use economic control and intimidation together. They may make bold comments such as, "If you don't get in line, you'll be out on the street!" Or, they may tease their victim by showing them bank statements or wads of cash and letting them know they won't have access to this money unless they do XYZ. In addition to controlling how funds are used, abusers may also ruin the credit of their victim, thereby making it nearly impossible for them to purchase a home, car or apply for a loan.

Although abusers may not directly steal or prevent access to funds, the effects of abusive relationships, both psychological and physical, prevent victims from showing up to work. It's estimated that a collective 8 million days of work are missed annually as a result of abuse. This results in victims being fired from their jobs and being unable to support themselves outside of the relationship.

Economic abuse is also prevalent within the family. Parents who are emotional or physical abusers may use economic control to prevent their children from earning their own money. By not adequately preparing them for the real world, they force their children to rely on them, setting them up for codependent habits as they grow older.

Minimizing Actions and Playing the Blame Game

Gaslighting is a popular tactic used by those diagnosed with narcissistic personality disorder. They will often avoid blame or misrepresent situations of verbal or physical abuse. This behavior goes far beyond accidentally forgetting small details. It is a purposeful strategy that makes the victim question their experience. One prime example of gaslighting is, "You're remembering that wrong, I never said that." In that instant, the severity of the abuse is questioned, thus making the victim wonder if they're just "overreacting." Stephanie Sarkis, author of the book Gaslighting: Recognize Manipulative and Emotionally Abusive People-and Break Free describes a gas-lighter as someone who, "Really gets under [the victims] skin and starts making [the victim] question [their] self-value."

Because the victim is afraid of the abuser, they begin to believe the stories they're being told. The victim may lose the ability to think rationally, thus entering a state of delusion. Their inner voice begins to take on the form of their abuser which makes them question everything about themselves. A formerly confident person can become so weighed down from the effects of gaslighting that they transform into a shell of themselves. Victims may struggle with connecting with others and expressing their true selves due to their low self-esteem.

Unfortunately, the effects of gaslighting flood into the victim's everyday life away from the abuser. Since they are conditioned to believe that their train of thought is wrong, they may have a hard time making independent decisions. Choosing clothing, food or even weekend plans may seem like a daunting task.

Minimizing is an off-set of gaslighting that makes the victim believe their feelings, dreams or needs are invalid. For example, if a victim presents a situation of abuse, a minimizer will say something to the effect of, "You're overreacting. Just get over it." This immediate disregard for the other's feelings leaves victims feeling insignificant and oftentimes, worthless. This proves that the abuser stops at nothing to make their victims feel as if their feelings are invalid. Throughout the relationship, minimizing transcends to non-abuse related topics such as discussing personal goals or dreams. An abuser who minimizes may completely disregard their victim's expressions by interrupting them, changing the subject or insulting them.

Finally, playing the blame game is one of the most cunning tricks abusers use to keep their victims within their reach. This, unfortunately, occurs in both physical and emotional instances of abuse. The abuser may say, "I wouldn't have to hurt you if you didn't behave the way you do." Or, "Because you did XYZ I had to cut off your expenses for the week." This form of abuse strips the victim of their power and makes them second guess their actions. They may begin to truly believe that their actions warrant the abuse they experience; almost as if they're deserving of mistreatment due to their mistakes.

Using Children as Pawns

Often, abusers use children to gain control over their victims. Gaining sole custody and eliminating all connection between the child and the victim is what drives the abuser. They'll make the victim seem unfit both publicly and privately. Or, they'll use economic status to gain custody over the children. This is especially prevalent when the victim is enduring economic control.

Abusers will also use the children as messengers by possibly forcing them to relay threats, coercions or apologies as a means to gain control over the victim. Also, abusers may take advantage of court-mandated visitations. Instead of focusing on time spent with their kids, they may taunt or insult the victim. This creates a tense environment for both the victim and their children.

The issue with this form of power and control is that it sows the seeds of abuse within each child. As mentioned, children who are exposed to abuse or violence are more likely to develop unhealthy habits such as mimicking abuse as they get older. Therefore, when abusers involve the children, they're simply putting gas into a never-ending vehicle of abuse.

Isolating the Victim From Their Family and Friends

An abuser's main goal is to keep their victim under

their spell. They know that if their victim expresses their concerns to friends and family members, they'll soon be exposed for who they are. As a result, they isolate their victims from their family and friends.

This isolation may start as subtle comments about the victim's friends or family members. "Your mom is so overprotective, don't you think?" is a common way to plant the seed of doubt within the victim's mind. Soon, the abuser will take those sly comments and turn them into blatant commands. They may prohibit the victim from spending time with their loved ones or completely monitor all forms of communication. This not only drives a wedge between the victim and their family, but also shapes how the victim perceives those around them. Let's uncover why.

As mentioned earlier, victims of abuse, especially psychological or emotional, suffer from irrational thinking. As their psyche has been manipulated and tainted for x amount of years, they are unable to decode right from wrong. When their abuser makes a blatant comment about their friends or family members, the victim doesn't have the mental capacity to combat that. Instead, their perspective is warped and shaped by the abuser's opinion. Therefore, they may begin to believe exactly what the abuser is saying about their said friend or a family member. The victim is then coerced into pushing their loved ones away by their abuser. Sadly, many victims don't even realize this is the abuser's intent until they are left isolated.

Another way the abuser isolates their victim is through guilt trips. For example, if a woman wants to spend time with her father, the abuser may say something along the lines of, "You always spend time with him and you never spend time with me." This blatant statement attacks the victim's character while presenting signs of jealousy and control. The victim is now trapped in the tangled web of guilt and blame. They may feel responsible for their abuser's insecurity. In turn, they may decrease the amount of time they spend with others and dedicate that time to their abuser.

Also, jealousy plays a huge role in an abusers MO. If they feel threatened by their victim's associates, they may begin to falsely accuse the victim of erratic behavior. The stress caused by these constant accusations may prompt the victim to remove themselves from outside contact to avoid an argument.

Emotional Abuse

Nearly 50% of both men and women in romantic relationships will experience some form of emotional abuse within their lifetime. This mind-numbing attack on a person's character leaves deep scars that are hard to mend. Let's consider why.

Emotional abuse is an ongoing attack of a person's appearance, character, values or more. This may involve name-calling, insensitive jokes, mind games or guilt trips. Often, this form of abuse is so subtle, the victim is unaware that it's happening until they stumble upon a helpful resource. One popular journal coined emotional abuse as "the silent killer."

Emotional abuse begins with the abuser picking at the victim. This could begin with slight jabs to their weight or manner of dress. Over time, these seemingly nagging hits turn into all-out accusations of character. The abuser may result in resort to calling the victim weak, overly emotional, a liar or insecure. This leaves the victim powerless and desperate for the abuser's approval. Deep down, they know they aren't these terrible things. However, their mind has been so warped to believe the abuser's accusations, they wind up believing everything they say.

Emotional abuse is sometimes just as hurtful as physical abuse. Some scholars have found that the scars of emotional abuse last longer than those suffering from physical violence. One noteworthy psychologist stated, "Responses to emotional trauma can result in disruptions in beliefs about oneself, relationships and the world." Much like the isolation tactic, the victim is so wrapped up in this warped perception of oneself, they're unable to reveal their true character. As a result of this ongoing attack on their character, they may find it hard to connect with others as they may start to believe the very things their abuser said about them. Over time, this constant exposure to negative self and outside talk leads to depression, anxiety and in severe cases, suicide. Victims of emotional abuse also have a hard time trusting others, even after they've gained liberation from their abuser. Since they've spent X amount of time being constantly criticized, they may believe everyone feels perceives them with the same eyes as their abuser. Thus, they're afraid of making real connections.

What Are the Long-Lasting Effects of Abuse?

Mental Health Disorders and Disrupted Brain Function

A recent study published in the American Journal of Psychiatry studied the brain of 28 women who were victims of sexual abuse in their formative years. Their goal was to determine if sexual abuse let to any physical changes in the brain's structure. After completing a thorough questionnaire, the women took a comprehensive brain scan. What the researchers found proved their hypothesis to be valid.

The 28 women who experienced sexual abuse housed a thinner somatosensory cortex in comparison to the neurological standard. This is an important part of the brain which controls how the body responds to and perceives physical touch. Jens Pruessner, associate professor of psychiatry, stated, "[Thinning] is associated with a lowered pain threshold. You would more easily perceive pain instead of touch." Because of this, women who have suffered from sexual abuse may perceive a simple touch as something threatening. This may raise their cortisol levels resulting in anxiety.

Another recent study from Harvard Medical School found a stark connection between verbal abuse and brain communication. They found that communication between the left and right hemispheres in the brain was non-existent in young people who suffered from verbal abuse. This broken connection opened the door for anxiety, disassociation, and depression. To cope with these challenges, many young people turned to illicit drugs.

In emotional or psychological abuse, the long-term consequences vary from person to person. Since victims spent the majority of their time being put down, ridiculed or controlled, they may experience difficulty with self-value and decision making. They may feel confused or apprehensive when taking steps towards progression. They may even feel guilty for certain decisions years after the abuse is over.

Fear is another common emotion that victims of physical and emotional abuse suffer from. From the physical perspective, they may fear getting involved with others because of their trauma. From an emotional perspective, they may struggle with trusting and opening up to others. As a result, they isolate themselves for extended periods of time. That fear can also manifest itself into low self-worth. Instead of feeling well-equipped and capable, they may feel worthless, unmotivated or blocked from making substantial changes. This, unfortunately, prevents many survivors from successfully moving past their experience.

To further prove this point, researchers have also found a huge connection between Post Traumatic Stress Disorder and physical abuse. An abuser could easily be trigged by household objects, television programs or even scents that remind them of their past abuse. To deal with these issues, some resort to detachment and disassociation. This is an unhealthy coping mechanism that victims use to separate themselves from the abuse and refocus their attention on something else. Unfortunately, detachment and delusions can lead to serious psychological troubles that impact the victim's ability to associate with the real world.

The Inability to Develop Lasting Relationships

Disrupting the pattern of abuse is extremely difficult when it comes to making friends or getting involved with others. While some victims may distance themselves from making connections, others may jump into the arms of everyone they encounter to fill an internal void. Unfortunately, this impulsivity could lead to the same pattern of developing toxic relationships with the wrong people. Ironically, abusers tend to have a subconscious radar of those they can take advantage of. Therefore, if a survivor doesn't take the time to heal themselves, they're more likely to let another abuser into their life.

Drug and Alcohol Abuse

Victims of abuse are more likely to resort to drugs or

alcohol as a coping mechanism. A 2012 study concluded that "Individuals with deficits in skills relevant to modifying emotional reactions and tolerance for negative emotions use drugs in an attempt to manage negative or distressing states." This is especially prevalent in those who have suffered verbal or psychological abuse. Because they don't have the mental strength to effectively manage internal issues, they mask that pain with momentary bliss.

The Take-Away

Abusive relationships come in all shapes, sizes, and patterns. What remains consistent throughout is the abuser's need for control and the inability to properly regulate emotions. This leads many to wonder, "What goes on in the mind of an abuser?" More importantly, "What makes a victim remain in an abusive relationship despite the apparent clues?" As we continue this discussion, we'll explore the psychological and physiochemical characteristics of an abuser. We'll then dive deeper into the cycle of abuse and how this impedes the victim's decision making, thus making them stay longer than they should. But first, let's enter the complex world of the abuser and explore the reasons behind their actions.

Chapter Two:
Decoding the hidden
signs of abuse

Introduction

Friar Cherubino was a socialist during the Medieval period who cautioned men on how to treat their wives when they stepped out of line. Instead of expressing their frustrations, he encouraged husbands to beat their women for the greater good. He hoped that women who got out of line would soon learn the consequences of their disrespect through physical punishment.

This was the unfortunate reality for women in the 1400s. Friar Cherubino, a prominent figure in the establishment of marital laws in Europe, documented the aforementioned statement in his Rules of Marriage. This casual, yet diplomatic approach to handling conflict essentially gave men the "okay" to orally, physically and psychologically abuse their wives whom they viewed as property.n

In a sense, men during Medieval times were shaped to abuse. It's safe to conclude that without Cherubino's concept, men who had a predisposition to abuse, whether environmentally or biologically, would have exhibited these toxic behaviors on their own. However, because of his influence on the law, men who naturally wouldn't abuse were given the go-ahead to act violently.

This unfortunate reality speaks volumes to the concept of social and environmental influence on behavior. Men and women display behaviors of abuse because of influence in various forms. Contrary to popular belief, the exposure to abuse, physical or verbal, during childhood doesn't always equate to an abusive adult. Juanito Vargas, an advocate for victims of abuse, attributes several abusive behaviors on societal or socioeconomic influence. When asked about sexual abuse, he explains, "The normalizing of sexual violence that infiltrates our daily lives through movies, television, pop culture, and rhetoric [influences] us without us even realizing it." The following chapter will explore the various seeds that flower abusive behavior in great detail.

As a result of the aforementioned influence, several abusers display specific patterns that control their victims. As mentioned in the previous chapter, abusers don't begin their relationship being violent or hurtful. If they did, the likelihood of attracting others is slim.

Instead, they lure their victims with sweet and thoughtful gestures. As time goes on, they unleash their demons and show their true abusive tendencies. By this time, the victim is already emotionally involved. This makes leaving increasingly challenging.

There are subtle red flags displayed throughout the beginning of any relationship, romantic or platonic, that indicate abuse. In this chapter, we'll take a deeper look into the abusive tactics mentioned in the previous chapter and the behavior that falls under those categories. We'll then uncover hidden signs of abuse that are often mistaken for admiration towards the beginning of the relationship. Understanding these patterns is key to identifying abuse and taking steps towards leaving the situation.

Common Behavioral Traits of an Abuser

The quintessential abuser portrayed in film and literature is male, powerful and undeniably charismatic. His smooth words cut like butter, but taste so sweet. Women are initially drawn to this archetype because they feel special or protected. Such traits are common among infamous serial killers and cult leaders. Let's consider a few. Charlie Manson was well-known for his charm and ability to make women feel good. Ted Bundy's strikingly handsome demeanor and "boy next door" appeal lured dozens, perhaps hundreds of women to their untimely death. Jim Jones, a famous cult leader of the 70s, made his followers swoon with his sweet words and promises.

You don't have to be a true-crime buff to know these men were notoriously abusive to the highest extent. However, their initial charm is what drove vulnerable victims to their demise.

The everyday abuser may not have a cult following like these villains. However, what they do have in common with those like Manson and Bundy is their ability to relate to people. An abuser knows just what to say at the perfect time. Their charm is what masks the beast that lives within. During conversations, they'll make their victims feel wanted, special and attractive. Excessive compliments or lavish gifts may even play a role in winning the victim over. These initial acts of love may even make the victim feel like they've hit the jackpot.

While several abusers take on the suave, powerful character. Others take on a completely different archetype. We'll refer to this character as The Vice King/Queen. This person comes across as gentle, perhaps soft-spoken and shy. They may watch their victim from afar, possibly waiting for them to make the first move.

Over time, this archetype bonds with their victim over common trauma. Perhaps they both came from unloving families or suffered abandonment at a young age. Instead of assisting their victims in the healing process, they take advantage of them. They'll use manipulative tactics to control their victim's behavior. This includes playing on their insecurities, guilt-tripping or tempting them with drugs or alcohol.

This abuser may also play the hero-card. Examples of this may be, "You're nothing without me!" Or, "If it weren't for me, you'd still be in your old, crappy position. You should praise me for rescuing you." This makes the victim second-guess their abilities and become extremely co-dependent. Unfortunately, the psychological effects of this type of manipulation are long-lasting and take years to overcome.

Whether the abuser is a charming Charlie or a Vice Queen, they all display a compilation of specific traits used to control and ultimately break down their victim. We'll now consider these actions in detail and highlight how their behaviors go from attractive to abusive.

Playing the Blame Game

Blaming is a deflecting tool used by abusers to bounce responsibility off their shoulders and on to someone else. It's a manipulative tactic that makes their victims either second guess their behavior or take on scrupulous amounts of guilt. This outright refusal to take responsibility for their behavior often manifests itself in unhealthy comparisons. Unfortunately, this is one of the hidden red flags that initially draws victims in.

An abuser may say something along the lines of, "You're nothing like that crazy man/woman I dated before." This subtle statement makes the victim feel special- almost as if they're seated on a throne. Sadly, this tactic is yet another scheme in the manipulator's plot to deflect responsibility.

As the victim gets deeper into the pits of abuse, the abuser no longer uses those "thoughtful" comparisons to make their partner swoon. Instead, they'll deflect-blame by convincing the victim of their wrongdoing. Let's consider this illustration.

A husband and wife are out enjoying a night out with friends. As the drinks keep flowing and the energy rises, the husband begins to flirt with a random waitress. Naturally, the wife is offended and decides to correct the matter respectfully. Instead of owning up to his mistake, he instead places blame on the wife. Comments like, "You're too sensitive" or, "Maybe if you did X more often, I wouldn't have to look for Z." A non-abusive husband would consider his wife's concerns and reflect on his behavior. They would engage in a conversation as opposed to mounting a verbal attack and hopefully find a lasting solution.

Abusers blame their victims for two reasons. One, they never learned how to effectively receive criticism. A simple, "I don't like when you do XYZ" is misunderstood as, "I don't like you as a person." They don't understand the difference between character and actions. Because of this unfortunate learning curve, abusers take even the slightest bit of criticism as an attack on their character. Their coping mechanism is to throw hurtful jabs at their victim to get even. Deep down, this slight comment is a jab at their ego – which sends them into an internal rage.

Two, abusers blame because they truly have no concept of personal responsibility. This is evident in those who fall under the spectrum of Narcissistic Personality Disorder. They are disconnected to feeling empathy or compassion for the feelings of others. Because of this, they display an air of superiority and demonstrate outright refusal to try and understand how their actions impact others.

The blame game causes an undue amount of stress on the victim's psyche. Over time, they'll begin to question their actions and behavior. After being convinced that they're too emotional, too sensitive, or completely overreacting, they may view themselves in that way. This results in low self-esteem and a completely warped sense of self-value.

Extreme Jealousy

Jealousy, within reason, is healthy. It shows your partner that you care and value them as a person. However, when jealousy goes from cute to extreme, the levels on the abuse meter are bound to skyrocket.

Examples of severe jealousy may range from forbidding someone to speak to a member of their sexual preference to physically following someone to see what they're up to. These jealous traits are invasive and may leave victims feeling vulnerable and exposed. In extreme cases, an abuser may force their victim to leave any situation in which they feel uncomfortable. When done in public, the victim may feel embarrassed for both themselves and their partner.

Jealousy is rooted in insecurity. Unless the abuser is a diagnosed narcissist or psychopath, those insecurities run rampant in their self-perception. Because they feel worthless, they may fear their victim will leave them for someone else. In some cases, the abuser may accuse their victim of infidelity to cover their own mistakes. By projecting their insecurity, they may feel as if they're compensating for their bad behavior.

When jealousy goes unchecked for an extended period, it could turn into psychosis. Psychology Today defines this state as, "Losing touch with reality." The abuser may believe hallucinations or made-up scenarios in their mind. This causes them to take their aggression out on their victims. In extreme situations, the abuser may lose all sense of morality. This causes them to behave erratically, causing harm or injury to their victim without even knowing the abuse is taken place. Fortunately, only about 3% of the population will deal with psychosis on this level.

Jealousy, when left to fester, grows into a monster of an emotion. Sure, everyone wants to feel desired by their partner. In some cases, a little jealousy can be attractive. However, it's best to keep an eye out when those cute, jealous comments transform into controlling and manipulative behavior.

Superiority Complex

Have you ever been friends or dating someone who thought the world owed them everything? The slightest inconvenience could send them into a babbling rant about why they deserve exceptional treatment. Although not every entitled person falls under the category of abuse, it's still important to note this common behavioral trade that several abusers share.

Bad times hit everyone at one point or another. It's the circle of life. Healthy individuals understand that, and while they may suffer due to an unforeseen occurrence, they usually don't believe unfortunate events are a personal attack on them. Take for example receiving the wrong order at a restaurant. An average person, while being slightly unnerved, may find a glimmer of understanding in this dilemma. The cooks may be having a hard day or the waiter may have misheard the order are typically normal responses. A person who suffers from a superiority complex, however, has no concept of understanding. Instead, they'll believe the cook, waiter or even the entire restaurant has a personal vendetta against them. This causes them to attribute every horrid thing and minor inconvenience they've ever experienced to someone disliking them. What an inflated sense of self!

An abuser, on the outside, carries themselves with an illusion of grandeur. They believe the world and those in it have no basis to dislike them. The very notion that they could make a mistake is ludicrous in their eyes. This mentality impedes their ability to truly relate to others and bleeds into how they want those around them to treat them. Let's consider how.

A person with a superiority complex has no real concept of person-to-person variety. This means that they expect everybody to act, think and make decisions that align with their perspective. When they encounter those who are different to them, they judge their character harshly. One primary example of this is cleanliness. A person with a superiority complex may think their home, appearance, car or workspace is far cleaner than anyone else around them. Should they visit the home of a friend, and notice the slightest accumulation of dirt or debris, they may find a reason to write them off as dirty.

This also trickles into the perception of others. For example, let's consider superiority between peers. An abusive person with a superiority complex may feel like they're the only ones working hard and making the best career decisions. When a friend of the abuser loses their job and has a hard time finding another one, an abuser may write that person off as being lazy or stupid. In reality, the friend may genuinely have a difficult time finding employment. This plays into the abuser's inability to understand the plight of others.

While we all have certain ways of doing things, we don't expect every person on the planet to fall in line. We also know that it's healthy to have a strong sense of pride in how we carry out our business. However, the problem arises when those personal accolades turn into missiles that destroy others.

We mentioned a lack of understanding and judgment at the outset. The connection between these two concepts is powerful, especially for victims who don't know how to perceive their toxic partner or friend. Since those with a superiority complex have no real concept of understanding, they'll harshly judge others for mistakes they've made, even minor. However, when the abuser makes a mistake, they'll usually have some personal reason for their behavior that somehow makes what they did okay. They also expect their victims to understand their behavior and issue immediate forgiveness. Let's consider an example.

An abusive girlfriend was caught sexting an ex. The boyfriend found out and naturally was upset. After momentary remorse, the girlfriend says, "You know I have a sex addiction, why can't you just support me?" Then, to make matters worse, she says, "Why can't you just get over it? It's not like I had sex with him. You take things too seriously."

Let's pause right here. The problem with this statement is the casual nature of the girlfriend's approach. Firstly, she should demonstrate unprecedented sympathy for the feelings of her boyfriend. Also, she cannot expect him to forgive her right off the bat. Furthermore, she never took full responsibility for her actions. Instead, she made an excuse and expected complete understanding.

Now, let's move forward a few years. The same couple is out with some friends. The boyfriend, who is friendly with everyone, notices an old female friend who he hasn't seen in a while. He knows she's going through a rough time. So, he takes her aside to offer some comfort and support. The girlfriend sees this, gets enraged in jealousy, and tries to scuffle with the female friend. The boyfriend storms off leaving the girlfriend in shambles.

Once the girlfriend finds the boyfriend, she accuses him of being a cheater, expresses how embarrassed she is and even goes on to question his loyalty. When the boyfriend explains that nothing fishy was going on and issues an apology, she gives him the silent treatment as a form of punishment.

What is the difference between the girlfriend's mistake and the boyfriend's? It is the girlfriend's abusive behavior. She expected the boyfriend to instantly forgive her blatant act of infidelity. However, she crucified her boyfriend for his perceived disloyalty. Even after hearing his side of the story, she refused to understand it and stopped communication.

The abuser expects perfection from everyone around them, but not from themselves. This makes the victim constantly at their disposal. The term "walking on eggshells" is appropriate for this environment because the victim is constantly looking for ways not to anger the abuser.

What's at the core of this behavioral type? Insecurity. An abuser with an inferiority complex is secretly dissatisfied with themselves. To cope with this dissatisfaction, and make themselves appear better, they'll find everything wrong with others. Sometimes going as far as pointing out their imperfections to "correct" them. In reality, these individuals are trying to control something external because they have no real internal control.

Victims of this form of abuse may begin to second-guess their character. Since their partner or friend expects perfection from them, they may feel unworthy or not good enough. This leads to constant feelings of self-doubt and drastically decreases their self-esteem.

Some victims, however, may internalize their hurt feelings, resulting in them resenting their partner. This may also cause them to shut down both orally and emotionally. They may feel disconnected from their abuser because their true selves aren't being honored.

Intense Criticism and Comparison

Criticism is a common manipulative tool used by abusers to get their victims to behave, dress or make decisions that align with their perception. An abuser's criticism may begin seemingly innocent. Such comments like, "I like it when you wear your hair down" soon turn to, "I demand you wear your hair down or I won't be seen with you." Amid that criticism is coercion and manipulation; the two underlying tactics of emotional abusers.

Some abusers use sarcasm or back-handed comments to hurt their victims. Statements like, "You look good in that suit considering all the weight you've gained" is a ploy used to make the victim feel down on themselves without giving them a solid basis for complaint. Psychology Today describes those comments as, "a temporary ego gain or some strategic advantage in a negotiation".Is it essentially saying, "I want you to do XYZ so I'm going to mask that request in a personal jab."

Sarcasm also comes in the form of belittling a person. Using a condescending tone to make your friend or partner feel stupid is a common tactic that abusers use to appear more intelligent and worthy of praise. Often, these sarcastic comments are so subtle, the victim may believe their abuser is trying to help them. Some examples are, "I can't believe you didn't know that. I would have thought you would know these things at this age." Not only is this comment disrespectful, but it is also treating the victim like a child.

We mentioned the concept of comparisons earlier. However, we didn't take a deep dive into the psychology of this form of abuse. As mentioned, an abuser may initially compare their victim to those in their past to elevate their egos. However, as the abuser grows comfortable with the victim, they may resort to unhealthy comparisons. The seemingly minor, "You aren't as fun as your friend Sally" could eventually turn into, "Why aren't you as good as a wife as your sister. You fail at everything in comparison to her."

The problem with unhealthy comparisons is that they make the victim feel inadequate or not good enough. This unfortunate tactic follows the victim even years after the relationship. They may struggle with feeling worthy of being in a relationship with someone else due to the years of verbal abuse.

Pathological Lies and Deception

Andrew Cunanan, the assassin of the late designer Gianni Versace, was a well-known king of deception. He made up elaborate stories of his upbringing and life experiences to make himself seem exclusive. Throughout his life, he demonstrated signs of extreme physical abuse, manipulation, and coercion. To this day, no one who spent time with him truly knows who he was as a person.

Deception is a common tool that manipulators use to influence people and win their approval. Abusers will lie about seeming small things such as, what they ate for breakfast, where they went to school and even who they are friends with.

Towards the beginning of a relationship, an abusive person may pretend to be successful, religious or family-focused. As the relationship grows, the victim will see that everything the abuser wasn't truly everything that they said they were.

What's interesting about this tactic is the reasoning behind it. Often, abusers lie about things, experiences or traits that they wish they possessed. Instead of genuinely working to improve themselves, they'll lie and deceive those who already have what they want. This speaks to their growing insecurity and dissatisfaction with themselves.

Deception also manifests itself into leading a double-life. It isn't uncommon for an abusive person to have a separate life from their victim. These abusers are so good at deception that their victim may not find out about their hidden agenda until years after the relationship is over.

Exposure to deception makes learning to trust again difficult for surviving victims. They may struggle in connection with others due to their turbulent experience. In extreme cases, they may question their intelligence, perhaps wondering how they didn't catch certain signs prior.

Explosive Fighting and Extreme Actions

An abusive person has the power to evoke fear and intimidation without laying a finger on their victim. This is evident during routine arguments that escalate to explosive battles. As mentioned in the previous chapter, intimidation is a common tool used to control behavior. It is methodic and planned, almost like a villain in a cartoon. This strategic approach is chilling as it forces the victim to comply over an extended period of time.

The problem with impulsive, explosive behavior is that it typically creates lasting consequences for momentary, thoughtless actions. Some examples of this are burning personal items, breaking furniture, calling the police or causing personal injury.

While explosive fighting causes emotional and physical scars, there's another element of extremity that falls under the category of emotional abuse. This is the threat to suicide. Susan Forward, the author of Emotional Blackmail, coined the term FOG to describe this hurtful, and oftentimes scary, form of explosive behavior. Let's consider what each letter in this powerful acronym stands for and how the abuser uses this to their advantage.

Fear: Fear is adrenaline based and either moves us to action, inaction or evacuation. When a person is presented with fearful stimuli, their body responds accordingly. Those who are more inclined to cower in their fears are more likely to fall for the abuser's threats of suicide.

For example, an abusive husband and his wife get into a disagreement over something subjectively simple. To make his frustrations known, he'll say, "If I had a gun right now, I'd kill myself because you're making me so miserable." The wife, naturally fearful, submits herself because she doesn't want him to take his own life. The husband, probably narcissistic and equally broken, has no intention of suicide. However, because he knows this tactic will trigger a positive response for him, he'll use it to his advantage.

Obligation: One author describes obligation as, "An innate sense of community responsibility." This involves showing up for others when they require emotional, social or sometimes economical support. Because of our biological makeup, we may feel a sense of guilt when we can't fulfill our obligations to others. This is especially strong in those who suffer from low self-value or codependency.

The abuser will use obligation to get what they want. If the couple is religious, a husband may threaten salvation to a wife who doesn't want to have sex with him. To oblige to her "wifely duty" and avoid Godly shame, she complies.

Non-religious abusers use obligatory statements to get what they want. Statements like, "You're supposed to make me happy but you're ruining my life" are placing the responsibility of one's happiness on the other person. This makes the blamed victim feel like they're not fulfilling their role as a supportive partner.

An abuser who constantly threatens suicide may transform obligatory statements into actions. They may overdose on pills that they know won't kill them to get attention from their victim. Once the victim feels sympathy for them, they will not be inclined to leave. This fulfills the obligatory commitment to the community mentioned in the outset.

Guilt: Emotional abusers will use guilt trips to make the victim feel obliged to behave accordingly. Examples of this are, "If you loved me, you wouldn't do XYZ…" Or, an emotionally abusive mother may say things like, "Your family has done so much for you, why aren't you coming to their birthday party! You're so selfish."

Attacking the character of another to get them to change their behavior is coercive and abusive. Abusers who threaten suicide use guilt to their advantage. Statements like, "If you were a better boyfriend, I wouldn't want to kill myself" are commonly used to make the victim feel horrible about themselves and ultimately cater to the needs of the abuser.

Since FOG plays so heavily on guilt, commitment and obligation, this prevents victims from leaving. They truly believe their abuser will commit suicide if they leave or stand up for themselves. Unfortunately, this is only one tool in the box that abusers use.

Getting Even

An emotionally abusive partner takes the statement "sweet, sweet revenge" to the next level. If they're upset with their victim, they'll try and make them jealous with immature and hurtful actions. For example, an abusive girlfriend may cheat on her boyfriend because he behaved in a way she didn't like. This is most commonly seen in narcissistic abuse where the abuser will discard their victim to punish them. At the root of it all is control. The message the abuser is trying to send is, "I don't need you. I am better than you."

Common Signs of Abuse

Victims manifest their abuse in different ways. While some carry physical scars, others hold the weight of emotional injury. We'll now consider a few behavioral traits exhibited by both men and women who suffered from the many forms of abuse.

Physical

Individuals suffering from physical abuse may hold bruises, scars or gashes on their bodies. Some of the most obvious places are the wrists, lips, eyes or neck area. Meticulous abusers may strategically mishandle their victims in places unseen to the public. This includes the back, genitals or upper arm.

Physical Abuse

Because the signs of physical abuse can be seen, victims will do everything they can to hide them. This includes wearing more clothing, even in the heat of summer, flaunting sunglasses indoors or wearing more makeup than usual.

Also, victims of physical abuse may become more sensitive to loud noises or physical touch. For example, a woman who has a physically abusive boyfriend may flinch when someone accidentally brushes behind or in front of her. In some cases, these symptoms are a result of post-traumatic stress disorder.

Emotional Abuse

Symptoms of depression and anxiety are two of the most common signs of emotional abuse. Victims may lose interest in previously loved hobbies or activities. Their eating and sleeping patterns may change, thus resulting in them losing or gaining large amounts of weight. Persistent anxiety paired with a lowself-image may run rampant, making the victim second guess every decision they make. In some cases, victims may turn to unhealthy coping mechanisms such as illicit drugs or alcohol. This impairs their judgment and results in poor decision making.

In social settings, victims of emotional abuse may become more withdrawn, meek, or soft-spoken. It's almost as if their presence is forgotten. They may decline to attend social events and stay confined in their homes. This is especially troublesome for individuals who were previously outgoing and confident.

Verbal Abuse

Victims of verbal abuse may repeatedly apologize for actions that don't warrant an apology. They may pass up on great opportunities or downplay their abilities as a result of being put down. In the workplace, a formerly high-performing employee may show up late, miss deadlines, or display a poor work ethic.

What's interesting about abusive behavior and the

mind is that several victims feel increasingly insecure when their abuser isn't with them. Although they're suffering due to this person's actions, they still have a strong connection with them. Victims may become visibly uncomfortable when their abusers leave the room, almost as if they can't stand on their own without them. This is usually caused by the victim's dependence on the abuser's commands.

They may even try and protect their abuser when others make comments regarding their behavior. Downplaying controlling actions or blaming the abuser's wrath on outside stressors is a common tactic victims use to deflect attention. While they know they're being treated poorly behind closed doors, they want to uphold the appearance of a happy, healthy couple. This could be ego-based or fear-driven. Their abuser may threaten abandonment, taking their children or inflicting personal injury as a punishment if the victim talks to anyone about their situation.

How Abuse Changes the Body

It's no secret that outside stimuli have a major impact on biological health. When the body endures scrupulous amounts of stress, physiological and biological changes are bound to occur. So much so that formerly healthy individuals may develop chronic conditions that stay with them for a lifetime. Let's consider a few.

Musculoskeletal System

Exposure to stressful stimuli has drastic effects on how well your muscles function. Often, chronic tension settles within the musculoskeletal system, causing persistent pain. This comes in the form of headaches, tension in the back or shoulders, along with undue pressure on joints. When individuals are exposed to this form of stress consistently, chronic conditions like fibromyalgia have a higher chance of developing.

Respiratory System

Another prominent area of the body that's impacted by stressful stimuli is the respiratory system. Exposure to abuse, both physical and emotional, creates a blockage within the throat, trachea, and lungs. This results in shortness of breath and difficulty breathing. In extreme cases, asthmatic attacks are triggered, causing the body to go into a state of shock. Other chronic conditions such as bronchitis, chronic obstructive pulmonary disease and emphysema are also common among abuse victims.

Cardiovascular System

Chronic stress creates tension within the cardiovascular system, causing victims to develop heart palpitations, hypertension and in extreme cases, stroke. This is especially evident in those dealing with constant emotional and psychological abuse. Also, victims of physical abuse may experience inflammation in their coronary arteries. When this part of the cardiovascular system is compromised, the risk of having a heart attack is increased.

Gastrointestinal Complications

The stomach is known as the "second brain" of the body. Several emotions such as fear and anxiety manifest themselves deep within the gut. Often, individuals exposed to high levels of abuse experience chronic stomach aches, issues with digestion and food sensitivities. This is one of the main reasons why individuals suffering from abuse experience no appetite and weight loss. Since stress settles so deep within the central nervous system, digestion is compromised and often causes frequent and consistent regurgitation.

Sexual Dysfunction

As mentioned, stress plays a major role in how well the nervous system operates. Since reproductive responses such as arousal and pleasure are regulated by areas of the nervous system, it's safe to assume the connection between reproductive dysfunction and abuse is strong. This is especially rampant in men suffering from abuse. Those exposed to severe levels of stress are known to have high levels of cortisol in the brain. The presence of excess cortisol impedes reproductive response, thus making arousal excruciatingly difficult for male victims. Their physical ability to feel arousal and pleasure is governed by their lowered sexual drive. Due to this, men who experienced a healthy sex life may lose their will to engage in sexual activity. Over time, this could even impact reproduction in general, making it difficult to conceive.

In women, similar effects are found. Some of the most common are skipped or infrequent menstrual cycles. This, parried with frequent stomach cramps could leave many women believing they are pregnant. Also, a lack of sexual desire and trouble with arousal may increase due to the high levels of cortisol within the body. Unfortunately, for women, this lack of interest in sex could bring on further sexual, psychological or physical abuse within their relationship.

Pregnant women suffering from abuse must be extremely careful not only for their health but also for the health of their child. Exposure to high levels of stress could lead to complications during pregnancy and labor and may even induce a miscarriage.

Common Treatment Options for Victims of Abuse

Once victims of abuse leave their abusive relationship, the real healing begins. They must learn how to properly understand the lengths at which they were abused during their relationship. Several victims seek refuge in peer-to-peer support groups. By explaining their experience with likeminded individuals, they're given the support they need to rebuild the pieces of their lives. These groups are also filled with men and women who can offer guidance, counsel and specific resources for recovering after abuse.

Finding these groups may be challenging at first. However, access to these groups can be found online or via non-profit organizations. Victims need not worry about their experience being shared publicly as these groups typically have a strong privacy policy.

In addition to community support, victims find the support they need through counseling or therapy. Cognitive Behavioral Therapy and talk-therapy are two of the main approaches therapists use to help their victims recover. Let's look at how and why these approaches work.

Cognitive Behavioral Therapy

CBT is commonly used for individuals trying to overcome trauma or neurological disorders. This approach is based on exposure and sorting through difficult situations head-on. Typically, a trained therapist will re-expose their clients to the past trauma with the goal of "normalizing" the situation. By doing so, the client can analyze their experience without the burden of emotion dictating their recovery. Besides, this also educates the client on how to not let their fearful memories dictate their behavior. Therefore, if the experience is triggered by their surroundings, they won't allow those triggers to scare them.

CBT also helps victims become more assertive in their dealings with others. Some aspects of assertiveness training are identifying and expressing needs, goal-setting and creating lasting boundaries. These tools are crucial for survivors of domestic abuse to have because it lessens the chance of future abuse.

Talk Therapy

Talk therapy is one of the most effective and traditional forms of therapy available. This allows survivors of abuse the opportunity to disclose information regarding their experience in a safe space. This is important because they probably have never had the opportunity to express their experience to someonewithout judgment before. As the therapeutic sessions continue, the therapist will give the victim strategic plans to help them leave their current situation or rebuild their lives. Often, they're given resources to housing, lawyers or other necessary channels.

It is the therapist's responsibility to report situations of physical violence. Because victims are usually apprehensive about going to the police, this ethical responsibility forces the abuser to pay for their actions.

Several victims of abuse find alternative coping mechanisms helpful during their road to recovery. Such include art therapy, meditation, yoga and Reiki healing. Meditation, for example, is an excellent tool for control and stress management. This works wonders for survivors dealing with the effects of depression or anxiety from an abusive relationship.

Is There Help for the Abuser?

All hope isn't lost for an abuser who wants to change. The imperative phrase here is, wants to. If an abuser wants to change their life course, there are several resources available for them to take advantage of. Often, abusers who use physical violence as a means of control are mandated by law to take specific classes disclosing the long-term effects of their actions. During these classes, the abuser will seek to uncover the underlying cause of their anger. These classes are specifically designed to give the abuser insight and clarity into their behavior and will help them understand how they have hurt their victims.

One of the main tenants of recovery for an abuser to understand is proper conflict management. Several abusers never learned how to express their wants and needs healthily. A trained therapist will give them the tools they need to effectively deal with conflict without resorting to verbal or physical abuse.

Exposure therapy is also effective for abusers as it forces them to own up to their actions. One domestic violence program for abusers in North Carolina begins each session with a report on someone who died from abuse. They analyze the parameters surrounding the death and may even show the abuser photos if they are available. By exposing them to this unfortunate situation, they can see the lasting repercussions of their actions.

The Take-Away

The signs of physical, emotional, psychological or verbal abuse are vast and can vary from person-to-person. Abusers are crafty and know how to hide their true intentions in a slick manner. Because of this, several victims are drawn to them, making the likelihood of abuse high.

As we continue in our quest for clarity on abuse, it's important to note that every action is rooted in something from the past. Our next chapter will discuss the unique mind of an abuser and why they behave in an unhealthy manner.

Chapter Three:
Understanding the Mind
of a Mistreater

Introduction

I don't know what happens to her when she gets angry! How can she act so normal as if nothing has happened? Can't she see how shocked and upset I am about the way she just behaved?

Verbal abuse can be just as painful as physical assault. And unfortunately, it is a real challenge to gauge what goes on in an abuser's mind before, during, and after inflicting pain on others. Even people who are the closest to him fail to understand the psyche of a mistreater fully. The psychology of an abuser is incredibly exciting, and at the same time, a complicated area of study.

They say, 'Violence is the first refuge of the incompetent.' But in many instances nowadays, we see that even highly successful people who have no history of abuse or deprivation resort to such distorted means for emotional catharsis.

A recent Australian survey on abusive relationships revealed that more than 15% of the adult Australian women population had experienced violence in some form or the other in their lives. And more than 60% of these abuses came from their partners or spouses.

In this section, we will dig deep into the underlying psychodynamics of an abuser's mind. We will evaluate their thoughts, emotions, and subconscious conflicts, explore why they believe violence can be the solution to any problem, and at what level does causing pain to others satisfy them.

The Driving Forces of Abuse

Dr. Lisa Fontes, an eminent mental health researcher at the University of Massachusetts, explained the psychological phenomenon of abuse as 'perspecticide' which is a combination of the words perspective and pesticide. She said that the sudden surge of impulses that happen during an act of violence washes away our preset opinions and thought patterns. This brainwash may come from an external provocation, drug or substance abuse, or an unresolved emotional problem, and acts as an eliminating agent that washes off all positive emotions that very moment. When the rage subsides, and the person regains his grasp over himself, he may feel sorry or find it hard to believe what he just did.

The emotional blundering associated with any form of interpersonal mistreatment is massive. Research shows that 2 in every ten children who seek mental health assistance have witnessed parental conflicts and domestic violence at home. What is even more disturbing is the way a victim's thought process changes after long-term exposure to such trauma and violence. Dr. Fontes mentioned in her research that if the abuse continues for years at a stretch, it changes the victim's self-perception and self-beliefs.

For example, a woman who has been tortured for years may start blaming herself. She might begin to think she has done something wrong that triggered her husband to act in the way he did. The phenomenon of *'Perspecticide'* then gets transferred from the abuser to the victim and the spectator of the scene.

Research indicates that any abuse crops from five primary sources. These are often the driving forces behind misbehavior, and sometimes also forms the basis of the one-sided dominance that prevails during most abusive relationships. Brutal people are guided by many negative thoughts and emotions, that are the root causes of most abuse and violence. The following 5 are the most predominant ones:

- Jealousy

Discrepancies in terms of looks, socio-economic status, or educational background might produce feelings of envy or jealousy in abusers. Abusers who fall prey to such negative ruminations may end up using them as a catalyst to their rage.

- Suspicion

Domestic violence growing from unhealthy suspicions about infidelity is a common thing and has been around for ages. Studies show that a majority of mistreaters have uncontrollable negative doubts and misgivings about their partners or their children. This ultimately causes them to go to the extent of controlling the victims' lives and ill-treating them for no good reason.

- Emotional insecurity

The one factor common to all abusers is their emotional insecurity which is mostly directed to the people who are closest to them. Vulnerabilities may be the result of traumatic experiences in childhood or an overall anxious nature. It creates trust issues and reduces resilience, which is why many perpetrators of violence are people with an uncontrollable fear of losing someone they love. They might forcefully isolate the victim to safeguard their irrational thoughts or coerce them to obey orders.

- **Egocentricity**

Some theories suggest abusers are selfish people at the core. They lack empathy and fail to look beyond their needs and gratification of impulses. An act of violence is often an act of self-protection for mistreaters. They lack the insight that their consequences can have actions. So, they cater to their temporary urges only, even if that involves someone loved getting hurt.

- **Past conflicts**

Most cases of violence have revealed that abusers have an unresolved past issue that got redirected as unhealthy aggression. For example, children who have been exposed to traumatic foster cares or have grown up with violent parents will most likely have an array of deprived childhood emotions. If these scars of early years do not heal with time, they get repressed and become unconscious conflicts. The result is low self-esteem and emotional instability, which shows up in brutal forms in adulthood.

The Vicious Cycle of Abuse

There is a typical pattern in abuse, especially the ones that come from close relationships. For example, most episodes of domestic violence start with a trigger, reach their heights, and then subside with a "Honeymoon" phase where the perpetrator acts utterly contrary to his violent nature.

This pattern goes on and off like a cycle, known as the 'Vicious Cycle of Abuse." There are five wheels of the abuse cycle -

- **The Build-Up Phase** - where the trigger

happens and is followed by a tense internal state.

- **The Standover Phase** - where the reaction begins and the verbal abuse increases.

- **The Explosion Phase** - where the ugliest form of abuse comes out. It is a violent outburst and in some unfortunate circumstances, can be fatal for the victim.

- **The Lament Phase** - where the abuser begins to understand what happened was not right but still does not have the insight to admit it was his fault. He might blame the victim, the surroundings, or other people for the attack.

- **The Honeymoon Phase** - where the mistreated may shower words of apology, love, and care, and pretend as if there is no problem at all.

The vicious cycle holds for most kinds of physical abuse. It does not always work for violence involving control and power play, for example, sexual abuse, verbal abuse, emotional blundering, and money shaming.

Women's Issues and Social Empowerment (WISE), an active non-profit organization in Australia, stated that *"Most domestic abuse occurs in relationships where conflicts arise from real or imagined inequality in partners. Perpetrators are usually the ones who feel threatened, which is why they resort to aggression for regaining their mental balance."*

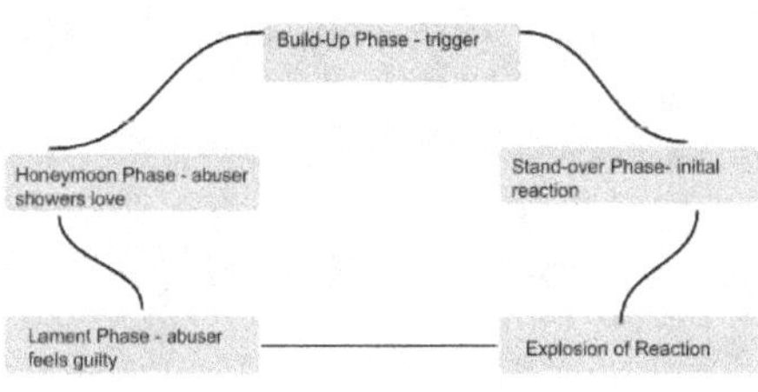

The Vicious Cycle of Abuse

What Goes Inside An Abuser's Mind?

It is challenging to attribute a singular cause to a violent action. Some mistreaters might be the most helpful person at home - a caring parent, a loving partner, and a reliable neighbor. But the moment they are triggered, the hidden monster comes out. Most perpetrators are similar to Jekyll and Hyde - they switch between starkly different personalities and confuse the victim altogether. While many findings suggest this to be an intended dichotomy, some studies indicate that abusers may suffer from dissociation or identity disorders *(Wilson and Butler, 2013)*.

Their Fear

Abuse is often an act of fear. Perpetrators of domestic violence, coercive control, or emotional maltreatment usually agree that their behavior is an act of terror, rather than rage. When talking about violence, we are concerned about what the victim's mental state is, with little thought given to what is happening inside the mind of the abuser.

What is it that abusers fear? Is the violence evidence of their shortcomings? Or does it depict an act of undoing?

There are no one-size-fits-all answers to these questions. Every abuser has a unique story and emotional experience that ultimately turns him to go down the wrong path. The most common sources of fear in an abuser's mind are -

- Fear of losing the victim (who is in a close relationship with the abuser).

- Fear of expressing weakness in front of the victim.

- Fear of being judged and mistreated. This can be the aftereffect of childhood trauma.

- Fear of being alone.

- Fear of losing power and control.

The abuser's act is often intentional and disguised, with the underlying fear being the driving force. How we can address these issues is a prime concern for mental health and social workers today (more on that in the following chapters).

Their Personality

Personality studies suggest five significant types and traits highly correlated with domestic violence and relationship abuse -

- Antisocial Personality

Antisocial personality traits can turn into an antisocial personality disorder, if not treated early. This explains an abuser's affinity to break the rules, their dependence on unfair means, the presence of a heightened sense of self, and their callous emotional perception.

- Borderline Personality

Borderline personality traits can cause an inclination towards harming oneself to cause stress and trauma to others. Mistreaters exhibiting this characteristic often slash themselves or give violent suicidal threats to get things done their way.

- Histrionic Personality

Histrionic personality disorder causes a strong need to be at the center of attention. The acts of violence are a way for the abuser to ensure that their partner prioritizes them and their needs before anything else.

- Narcissistic Personality

Narcissistic personality traits are a ubiquitous attribute in mistreaters. This calls for an inflated sense of self-worth and the inability to look beyond personal needs and gains. Perpetrators with such traits are sensitive to criticism; they force the victim to comply with their orders, even the most unreasonable ones.

- Sadistic Personality

Sadistic personal dispositioncharacterizes an unconscious pleasure from seeing others in pain. Abusers are unempathetic. They deliberately try to avoid any chance of them getting hurt, even if that means hurting someone else. The presence of sadistic traits makes them more intimidating, rigid, and difficult to persuade.

Physical violence is the only form of abuse that we can see with our eyes and measure with standard tests. There are no known ways to measure the damage caused by emotional abuse, psychological trauma, verbal abuse, and social harassment. What makes the scenario even worse is –

- The silence of the victims who do not want to lose their loved ones. Friends and family supporting the abuser and asking the victim to give them 'another chance.'

- Lack of evidence to prove what has been going on behind closed doors.

Are Abusers Manipulative?

Manipulation plays a crucial role in any form of abuse, especially the ones where the victim is a partner or spouse. Abusers can go to any length to manipulate the victim. To them, manipulation is the precursor to winning the game and turn things onto their side. The drive behind manipulation may be establishing a point, gaining and maintaining control, or boosting self-esteem by letting someone else down.

The means of authority that a manipulative mistreater uses is similar to B.F. Skinner's components of learning. Skinner's theory suggested that we learn either by a definite inclusion in our environment or a detrimental addition in an extreme scenario. His findings hold for manipulation in abuse as well. Most manipulators use one of the three following ways to overpower the victim –

- **Positive reinforcement** - including unending compliments and praises before an abusive attack. This also encompasses superficial affection, bribes, expensive gifts, or public display of affection (PDA).

- **Negative reinforcement** - whereby the abuser may remove something from the victim's personal space to make sure he gets it done his way. A classic example of negative reinforcement is an abusive husband who would not let his wife contact her parents until she submits to his unfair demands.

- **Punishment** - Punishment in an abusive relationship is manifested by shooting, beating, public humiliation, making rude comments about the victim's appearance to make her lose her sense of self-worth, blackmailing, or forced sexual contact. This is undoubtedly the most extreme and painful means of manipulating the victim.

Brainwashing - The Hidden Truth of Abuse

All her childhood memories circle around listening to how horrible she looks, how incompetent she is, and what a shame she has been for her family. And now she has grown up to be a person with shaky self-worth, lack of empathy, and reduced self-confidence. Her emotional insecurities devour self-love, and every time she tries to find love, she ends up being with the wrong person again!

Sadly, this is the future of many victims of childhood abuse. Studies have shown that most women who are victims of domestic violence have a distorted sense of self and are too scared to snap out of the relationship. They are also soon to blame themselves and have an ingrained mindset of 'making things up' due to their rageful partners.

Contrary to what we usually believe, abusers and their victims both suffer from a disoriented sense of self. Their self-esteem, self-love, and confidence worsen the situation, making them vulnerable to causing pain (the abuser) and withstanding the same (the abused).

Lundy Bancroft, in his famous work 'Understanding

the Batterer in Custody and Visitation Disputes' mentioned -

"Because of the distorted perception that the abuser has of his rights in the relationship, he considers himself to be the victim instead of the inflictor. This imagined helplessness then turns into self-defense. He views any refusal or disobedience as an act of aggression towards him, especially when it comes from the victim. He thus accumulates these negative experiences and perceptions and uses them as justifications to convince himself that what he did was in favor of his self-identity."

Whatever may be the form of the abuse, the basic structure remains the same. But the good news is, identifying these patterns of malfunctioning relationships can save the victim from losing himself/herself. Psychologists believe that recognizing if we are in a relationship with a potential abuser is easy. One factor common to all abusers is their inevitable motivation to 'brainwash' or convince the victim in their favored way.

Things may start by criticizing the victim's values, moral standards, behavior, and looks. For example, talking to the opposite sex may be pointed out by abusers as a sign of flirting, or even worse, infidelity. In a blink, these constant damaging comments and criticisms can become the victim's reality. They may start seeing themselves as what the abuser tries to show them, and share the delusion to make things worse.

The aftermath of brainwashing is devastating

Abusers use sharp logical reasoning to prove their point and alter the thought pattern of the victim to cause them to blame themselves. An abuser can use different means of brainwashing and controlling the victim's mind, some of which are -

Social Isolation

You may never know when you get isolated from your family, friends, and community if you are in an abusive and mentally taxing relationship. Abusers often force victims to believe that the only person who loves and cares for them are the abusers themselves. It may start off with the abusers feeling possessive about the partner giving someone more attention, and end up becoming as ugly as physical violence or emotional blackmailing.

Resistance

Resistance is when the abuser manipulates the victim to become so dependent on him, that he/she is not left with any other option but to tolerate the pain. In such cases, the victims are forced to believe that they cannot live by themselves. They feel that they 'need' the abuser for sustaining life, which ultimately reduces their ability to resist the violence and protect themselves.

Threats

Using threats as a mechanism to brainwash the

victim is extreme and frequently happens in case of physical violence. Threatening the victim causes them to experience anxiety, despair, and a strong sense of helplessness, especially if the victim is a teenager or a child. This is one of the biggest reasons why many cases of physical abuse stay masked forever. Victims are too scared to talk about it, lest it causes more pain.

Indulgences

Complying with any form of abuse - verbal, emotional, or social, can make it worse for victims to control it later. Abusers use such occasional compliances as a means to exert their will on victims. Speaking up on day one is always the best answer to abuse, even when it comes from a dear one.

Degradation

Degradation is the most popular form of brainwashing, where abusers force the victims to damage their self-esteem and make them perceive themselves as incapable. It may sometimes be a defense for the abuser, who is battling with his sense of self, but it jeopardizes the victims' motivation to protect themselves.

Cognitive and Emotional Basis of Abuse

The human mind works at three levels –

1. Cognition - what we think

2. Emotion - what we feel

3. Action - what we do

Abuse is usually the action; it is the consequence of faulty thinking and emotional perception. So, before managing the behavior, it is vital to understand the influences that caused it in the first place. The methods that male or female abusers use are part of their natural thought processes - they are tuned in to think and feel that way. Many abusers share a similar pattern of thought, which marks them as dysfunctional, insecure, and unable to sustain any long-term relationships.

They are unhappy unless they are in complete control of the victim - the reason being their underlying thought blocks and emotional barriers. There are five main cognitive biases or negative thought patterns that have been associated with acts of abuse –

- What is he/she thinking?

Presumptions are a common foundation in injurious and violent behavior. Recurrent anxiety over what others think and feel causes mistreaters to delusively read their minds and act as per what they believe is correct. It may be completely unrelated to what the victim thinks or feels, but it is a challenge to make an abuser understand this.

- I don't fit in

Abusers can suffer from an inferiority complex and

personal inadequacies. Constantly feeling as if they are not good enough creates stress, which, if left unresolved, may manifest as abuse and violence towards others.

- Personalization

Abusers are prone to taking things too personally. They can hold a grudge for years, and instead of resolving it rationally, they negatively channel the anger.

- Judgmental

Being critical or over-judgmental is a negative thought pattern that limits the power of rationalization. Core beliefs such as 'drinking makes a girl too easy'/'working women are not good mothers'/'income decides a man's power,' etc. are examples of judgmental NATs (Negative Automatic Thoughts) that often lie at the core of verbal or physical abuse.

- Black-and-white reasoning

Also known as all-or-none thinking, black-and-white reasoning is a typical example of a thought block present in the mind of an abuser. It is a destructive cognitive pattern that forces someone to believe that either something or someone is the best or the worst. Black-and-white reasoning explains the rapid switch from the explosion to the honeymoon phase as well. When angry, abusers fail to remember anything praiseworthy about the victim.Upon moving into the honeymoon phase, he finds the victim more lovable than ever.

Lack of emotional control is common in most abusers. They fail to regulate their emotions or acceptably express themselves. Abusers have low emotional intelligence. Daniel Goleman, an expert in the field of EI, said that the inability to understand what they feel, why they think so, and how they should talk about their feelings makes it worse for abusers. They prefer keeping everyone in the dark as they are unsure of how to speak out about what is going on in their minds.

There may be deep-rooted causes of the emotional struggle abusers face, but mostly it is linked to some cognitive distortion that has been left unresolved. Emotional instability is one of the driving forces behind substance abuse as well. Statistics indicate a positive correlation between substance dependence and violence. For example, many cases of rape and sexual abuse on women have been caused under the influence of stimulants or other drugs. There are arguments for and against the impact of substance abuse and violence, however, the fact that substance abuse causes emotional instability in abusers is undeniable.

Aggression - Dominant and Passive

There is no abuse without aggression, whether it takes the form of acting out or passively showing it. Passive aggression, also known as 'silent treatment', acts as slow-poison and is generally found in emotional abuse. It has long withstanding effects and is often hard to describe.

Aggression is a manifestation of anger - we show it by either yelling at the person we are angry at, or by bottling up the feeling and expressing it otherwise. For abusers, anger is the most dominant emotion that controls their actions.

Expressions of expressive aggression include -

- Shouting and cursing at the victim,

- Physical violence and attack,

- Using swear words and abusing the victim's family,

- Throwing and breaking things, causing damage to the household,

- Forced sexual intimacy,

- Malevolent acts of self-harm.

Passive-aggressive violence, on the other hand, is more subtle and painful. Examples of passive aggression include -

- Using subtle, ambiguous statements that make the victim feel sad or overwhelmed,

- Refusing to clarify conversations and an intentional lack of communication,

- Going without talking to the victim for days, which becomes more painful if the abuser is someone from the family or a close acquaintance,

- Displacing the anger to something/someone else, for example, refusing to eat, shouting at kids, or yelling at colleagues at work for no reason,

- Bringing up the past,

- Hitting on an argument for something petty, which is not the real reason for anger,

Identifying the pattern of aggression in an abuser can be a significant step forward to managing the mess early. We must understand that at some level, the pain abusers are inflicting on others is an attempt to reduce the burden they have been carrying themselves. Undoubtedly, they make the victims prisoners of their own lives, but the abusers too are trapped at some level. It may be a cognitive bias, an unresolved childhood trauma, a personality disorder, or emotional dysregulation, but decoding the underlying psychological conflict of an abuser's mind can go a long way in helping them and the victims to overcome the struggle.

Abusive relationships can change the victim's thought process completely. In many instances, victims, especially women, who face violence from their partners slowly start blaming themselves for provoking the abuser into abusing them. In psychology, we call this 'shared delusion.'

In one of her research works on the psychology of abuse, Dr. Lisa Fontes mentioned that:

"In an abusive and controlling relationship, it is mostly the abuser who determines what love is and what it is not. He may successfully persuade the victim to believe that torture is a supreme form of love, or obsession is another name for dedication. The mistreater manages and regulates how the victim thinks, feels, and interprets the episodes of violence."

Her idea of "perspecticide", as mentioned earlier, holds for these behaviors as well. She believes that this is how many mistreaters succeed in making victims disconnect from their friends and family, or even give up their financial independence.

Physical violence never comes alone. In most cases, it goes hand in hand with emotional and verbal abuse. Once the abuser begins his abuse, he will continue down that path without having the slightest realization of the pain he is inflicting on his close one.

The real question while trying to unleash the mind of an abuser is not the 'what' or 'why' of his actions. It is the knowledge of 'where' did the aggression and emotional dysregulation come from?

Focusing on their current actions and managing them is not the first step in dealing with abuse in hand. Digging into the roots of where it all started is where the intervention begins. For example, exploring areas such as:

- When was the first time he attacked someone?

- Was he angry as a child?

- Is there a genetic link?

- Has he learned this behavior at home?

- Has he seen others doing it?

- Is it some other underlying mental health condition that is causing this?

Psychotherapists dealing with domestic abusers or victims always keep a close check on the emotional ups and downs of an abuser. Studies have found that regular monitoring of how their thoughts and feelingsfluctuatesheds insight on the probable roots of abuse.

The act of violence may be quick and easy. But everything around it is complicated and worth researching. We had a look at the thoughts and beliefs that circle the mind of an abuser. In this next part, let us peep into what other psychological factors may contribute to someone becoming a mistreater.

Comorbid Conditions

It is not just the victim who gets injured in the violence. Any act of brutality has more than one person who gets hurt. If a partner gets abused, the child gets hurt too. If a young girl gets abused, her parents and family are also injured. The incident may be momentary, but its effects linger for a long time.

Theories suggest that violence may be a manifestation of an underlying mental health condition. Random acts of violence and attacks that happen on the streets are inflicted mostly by strangers and passers-by who have some comorbid psychopathology.

Mood disorders and impulse control problems are pervasive in abusers. Many female victims of domestic violence have reported that their mistreaters experience a sudden desire to attack, and anything she does during those moments can provoke him to cause pain. Once the mood swing subsides, everything goes back to normal for the abuser.

Depression and manic episodes are common psychopathologies associated with violence and abuse. Both these conditions manifest itself in forms such as:

1. Heightened irritability,

2. Being provoked in the absence of any arousing stimuli,

3. Insomnia,

4. Frequent mood swings with a rapid switch from a perfect mood to a terrible one,

5. Lack of impulse control,

6. Substance abuse or drug dependence,

7. Complete apathy or inappropriately high interest in social activities,

8. Abnormal libido.

Underlying depression, mania, or bipolar disorders arouses the sympathetic nervous system in the body, causing an increased fight-or-flight response. Constant activation of the fight-or-flight mechanism causes edginess and makes the abuser vulnerable to acting on it.

Physiological changes associated with such problems also include significant dysregulation of sex hormones and neurotransmitters such as adrenaline, dopamine, ACTH, and cortisol. Similar patterns are found in paranoid schizophrenics who mostly inflict torture to undo an inner discomfort or get rid of their suspicions. Other psychopathological conditions associated with domestic and other forms of violence include:

- Chronic stress

- Hypertension

- Anger problems

- Frustration

- Drug abuse

- Seasonal Affective Disorder (SAD)

- Atypical Depression

- Postpartum manic psychosis

- Delusional disorders.

Nurture Over Nature?

There are substantial arguments regarding the importance of nature and nurture in shaping an abuser's personality. Some theories suggest that upbringing, or the environment in which an abuser grows up and learns, plays a crucial role in determining the nature and intensity of the abuse.

Boys who grew up seeing their father figure abuse women in the house are more likely to acquire the same behavior to getting things done his way. On the contrary, girls who grow up seeing their mother getting abused are more likely to grow up having trust issues or experiencing emotional instability. They may unconsciously get driven to abusive partners and repeat the role their mother played and succumb to the abuse (Dutton, 1996).

Observational learning is another crucial psychological phenomenon for abuse. Learning theories suggest that the most reliable response pattern that a child acquires is by observing others respond to similar stimuli.

Violencecan come in several forms, from hair-pulling to name-calling to bullying or money shaming.Any behavior that is targeted towards upsetting or injuring an individual (physically, mentally, and emotionally) can be considered an abusive action.

An interesting fact about relationship violence is that

most abusers feel that they are powerless and inferior. Their aggressive mannerisms are intended to restore their so-called 'power' and regain emotional balance.

Here are some interesting facts about domestic and partner aggression that stem from associated psychological conditions:

- Most of the attacks take place behind doors when the victim is all alone and helpless.

- Mistreaters with a psychological condition rarely accept it or take responsibility for their actions.

- Abusers are quick to blame victims for provoking them.

- Physical violence follows verbal abuse.

- The abuser attempts to tarnish the victim's self-esteem.

- The abuser is over-sensitive and incapable of having a mature discussion.

- The abuser seeks refuge in drugs and alcohol before committing the misdeed.

A Psychological Profiling Of Mistreaters

Abuse is altogether a win-lose game for mistreaters. Whether or not they are suffering from a psychological condition, they perceive their actions as a deed of control over the victim. Most male abusers report deriving a

the situation.

EQ studies have shown that abusers with average or higher than average levels of IQ may still resort to violence. Their emotional restrictions overpower their mental faculties, and as a result, they fail to find an acceptable way of handling a dispute.

Lack of problem-solving skills in abusers often crop up from a prominent dichotomy in thoughts, or the negative automatic thoughts mentioned earlier in this chapter.

- Low self-esteem

Violence stems from low self-esteem and ultimately results in the same. Most cases of relationship abuse have revealed that abusers tend to have low self-esteem and self-confidence which they then regularly try to pass onto the victim. While the violence starts with an under-confident perpetrator, it often ends up creating a self-deprecating and under-confident victim.

- Emotional instability

Some recent reports on domestic violence revealed that many mistreaters felt 'emotionally secure' after inflicting pain on the victim. Abuse such as forced sex and physical injury are, in most cases, an effort to ensure that the victim is weaker and incapable of retaliating.

Abusers feel lonely all the time. They are known to have fewer friends and are always jealous and unhappy if their partners pay more attention to anyone else. Some extreme cases of domestic violence have even recorded the perpetrator getting infuriated if the victim paid more attention to their child than the abuser.

Emotional dependence and lability are common mental blockages in abusers that mostly arise from early childhood experiences. Children who are bullied and have faced social isolation in their prime years are more likely to develop unhealthy emotional dependence later.

- Frustration over personal shortcomings

Many cases of relationship and family abuse occur when the mistreater is undergoing personal failures, such as unemployment or financial hurdles. Personality studies have shown that most abusers are inherently less resilient to stress and tend to be hyperreactive. They lose control over minor failures and displace their frustration on others to reduce their pain.

A classic example is a child who gets beaten up by his mother, who recently got divorced and is struggling to get a job. She would reflect her frustration and turmoil on her child by spanking or scolding him over petty things, thereby putting the mother-child relationship in danger too.

- Perceptual disorders

As they say, 'It is not about what we see, but how we see it."

Understanding the mind of an abuser starts with understanding the way they see the world and themselves. To a rational person, the best way to deal with a relationship issue is to talk about it, argue over it, and ultimately come to an understanding. However, for an abuser, the response starts with blaming, exerting power and dominance, and eventually wounding the victim. The underlying psychology behind this unreasonable action is the way the abuser interprets the situation.

The two-factor theory of emotional intelligence by Schachter-Singer (1962) stated that we get aroused by a stimulus at two levels - the physical level (hormonal surge) and the psychological level (the way we interpret and add meaning to it).

Negative perceptual patterns impact the psychological arousal related to an event, and as a result, the entire response pattern gets damaged. These malfunctions are tied in with cognitive roadblocks and are often managed by thought replacement or cognitive interventions.

- Pathological lying habits

Abusers are quick to deny their mistakes. Domestic abusers are also known to seduce their victims by lies and manipulation via masked statements. They can switch roles whenever they want to and are sometimes intelligent enough to leave no proof of what they have done.

Lying habits can be due to an underlying psychopathology. It is not always a sure-shot indicator of abusive tendencies, but it does have strong associations with violent personalities. It is difficult to rule out pathological lying from normal lying habits, but common symptoms include:

- An overall egoistic and self-centric thinking pattern,

- Lying over small things that can easily be overlooked,

- Constantly blaming others for things that they have not done,

- Playing the 'victim' role at all times,

- Yelling and being violent to prove truthfulness.

- Why Do Victims Stay Back?

Unleashing the psychological aspects of an abuser's mind raises the obvious question - "Why do victims choose to stay with the mistreater even after knowing what is right and what is wrong?"

Stockholm Syndrome is one explanation of why some victims cannot leave the abusive relationship that they are in and move on with their lives. The presence of a shared delusion and experiencing repetitive dominance somehow coerce the victim to believe that he/she cannot survive without the violent partner. Studying the reasons behind long-term abusive relationships is as complicated as understanding the psyche of the wrongdoer.

Some other reasons why victims stay back in an abusive relationship include -

- Presuming that the abuser will get hurt if he/she leaves.

- Fear of other family members getting harmed by the abuser.

- Low self-confidence and lack of self-reliance, which makes the victim think that he/she cannot survive alone.

- Anxiety about significant life changes.

- Blaming oneself for torture.

- Delusion that he/she can save the abuser from self-destruction.

- Financial instability or economic dependence on the abuser.

- Social or cultural barriers.

- Lack of knowledge and awareness about violence and abuse.

- Fear that no one will trust the victim.

- Worry over child custody and associated legal hazards.

- Emotional attachment to the batterer that makes

the victim unconsciously justify the abuse.

- A strong belief that the abuser will change and that this is the last time he/she is inflicting pain.

- Physical ailment or other conditions.

Other Psychological Phenomena Inside An Abuser's Mind

There can be a combination of thoughts and feelings that contribute to an abusive personality. Some significant psychological factors common in most abusers are -

- Lack of self-esteem

Poor self-esteem is one of the prime reasons as to why abusers are indecisive and overly sensitive. They find degrading and insulting others satisfying in a way as it makes them feel more valuable and heard. Lack of self-esteem in perpetrators can exist singularly or with associated issues such as a fear of failure, a negative body image, hyperactivity, hypersexuality, etc.

Abusers who lack self-esteem are likely to:

- Believe that they are being ignored and criticized.

- Draw all attention to themselves by inappropriate behavior and over-connectedness. They may call ten times a day and send a hundred messages to the victim to ensure that they are remembered and well-attended.

- Feel better when the victims feel bad about themselves.

- Give false suicide threats when victims refuse to comply with their demands.

- Talk more and profess their love instead of reflecting on their feelings through their actions.

- Make the friends and family of the victims feel unwelcome when they are around the victims.

- Cyclical emotional conflicts

Mood charts of an abuser resemble sea waves; they rise and fall periodically. Just like the vicious cycle of abuse, the emotional world of abusers also fluctuates between being edgy and irritable to being loving and affectionate. Some abusers agree that they inflict pain to ease their inner discomfort. They lose control of their feelings and act out in ways that are unacceptable and unforgivable.

The emotional cycle of an abuser has the following facets:

- Ensuring their importance and control in the relationship.

- Extreme feelings of jealousy, possessiveness, and hatred.

- Manipulating the victim in every possible way to restore inner peace.

- Anger and frustration.

- Unreasonable claims and blaming the victim of abusing the perpetrator.

- Passive emotions reflected by self-harming, starving, quitting work, and substance abuse.

- Breaking things and insulting people related to the victim.

- Subconscious role reversal

Having a past connection with abuse is prevalent in abusers. Studies have pointed out that more than 40% of male domestic abusers have had a history of physical violence at home or in foster care facilities.

Often, victims of abuse (especially childhood abuse) turn out to become abusers as they grow up. Psychoanalytic research suggests that inflicting pain on others is unconscious method of coping with childhood torture. Children are usually helpless and have little option to fight any abuse in childhood. However, the negative emotions that come with the pain stay repressed and can show up in ugly ways later in life.

Some instances of abuse victims who are vulnerable to switch roles in the future and cause pain to others are:

- Individuals who had aggressive romanticor

marital relationships in the past.

- Individuals who were sexually abused in childhood.

- Children who faced parental neglect, especially from the mother.

- Children who faced physical abuse coming from their parents, teachers, siblings, or peer group.

- Individuals who were a silent witness of parental conflict and abusive mom-dad relationship.

Experiencing abuse doesn't guarantee that the victim will turn into a mistreater at some point in life. However, unresolved and unknown abusive experiences in childhood make a person more vulnerable to repeating similar behaviors under similar circumstances.

- Critical separation anxiety

Imagine a child who grew up with foster parents because his father left, and his mother is a drug addict in rehabilitation. How would the child have felt when he was forcefully taken out of his own house, denied the comfort of staying with his mum and dad, and forced to live with a couple who are strangers to him?

Nearly ⅔ adult abusers have a history of painful or forced separation early on in life. The loss of someone close during childhood may seem unendurable to kids as they cannot express themselves in relevant words like grown-ups.

The result of such coerced separation leads to deep-rooted anxiety and negative emotions, which cluster together to shape an abusive personality. While we may sympathize and show pity towards the child who is separated, we often fail to empathize with him when he starts abusing his partner.

Unaddressed separation anxiety acts as a catalyst in the disrupted mind of an abuser, resulting in:

1. An increase in the frequency and intensity of domestic violence.

2. A constant identity crisis.

3. Asking for continuous reassurance from the victim about marriage, moving in, and fidelity.

4. Marked discomfort at the thought of the victim moving out, relocating for a job, or choosing to live life on their own terms.

The psychology of an abuser is critical and intense - abuse is a collective outcome of several thoughts, emotions, early experiences, genetic links, and personality dispositions. But uncovering and exploring the mind of an abuser is vital in preventing and managing violence. Identifying early signs of abuse can help victims seek help early and save the relationship before it goes out of control. Thankfully, the social and legal standards against violence are very high today, which makes it easier for victims to raise voices and ask for support.

Chapter Four :
How to Leave the Abuser and Find Your Own Strength

Introduction

"Why can't she just leave him and move on in life?"

This is what most of us would think when we hear about someone in a violent personal relationship. Deciding to break loose from an unhealthy relationship is not a cakewalk, especially when it has multiple strings attached to it.

For example, in most cases of domestic violence on women, victims fear losing their social identity, child custody, or dragging their families into all the legal hazards. Women take years to even speak about their distress, and in most cases, they choose to stay in the relationship despite the torture.

Leaving an abuser is extremely difficult when the

relationship has been a long-term one or when the victim is entirely dependent on the abuser for their livelihood. A child who is molested and abused by his close family members may take years to speak up about the mishap and a lifetime to recover from it.

There is a famous Roman saying, which means "Children are like kites that parents keep tied with threads. If the threads are not on time, the kites would never learn how to fly alone." Learning how to combat violence at home and in close relationships is therefore vital to being able to ultimately break free of it.

This chapter will disclose some crucial points on standing against violence and tips to untie yourself from that fatal bond. We will have a look at what goes on inside the mind of a victim before taking the big step forward to see how we can prevent violence at its nascent stage.

Domestic Violence - Myths and Facts

The definition of violence and abuse often varies across cultures and other demographics. What may seem aggressive to us may be a ritual or a traditional custom for another group of people.

This diversity in the nature and characteristics of aggression has given rise to several beliefs that are not always true. To understand what violence is, we must be able to rule out what it is not. Here are some popular myths around domestic violence and abusive relationships that we should address to eradicate it from our lives.

- **Perpetrators of violence come from a lower socioeconomic background** - No, they don't. Abusers can come from any walk of life and be affluent or needy. Violence in any form is primarily a matter of a person's mindset more than anything else.

- **Victims provoke perpetrators** - It is rarely true. No provocation can be a good enough reason to be physically or verbally violent towards others. Anything can ignite an abuser due to his lack of impulse control.

- **Violence is genetic** - Violence is essentially 'nurture over nature.' There might be some evidence that suggests genetic influence in acquiring such behavior patterns, but it ultimately depends on our upbringing and mindset. We must remember that violence is an act of choice, not compulsion.

- **It is okay for men to be angry sometimes** - Anger is an emotion present in all human beings. However, we should watch out if our temper reaches to a point where we want to harm others. Acting out violently, under most circumstances, is a broken way of self-expression.

Inside the Victim's Mind

Young victims of violence, such as children, or newly married individuals, can be emotionally immature or lack foresight. They may find it overwhelming to suddenly leave the abuser. Studies have suggested that most victims who undergo separation from a torturous relationship engage in one or more of the following contemplations at some point.

- What should I consider before I decide to leave?

- Should I talk to anyone before taking the final step?

- How can I ensure my safety from now on?

- How do I manage my finances?

- How should I talk about it with my kids?

- Where should I go once I leave?

- Should I consider moving to a sheltered home?

- Can I get a job if I relocate to another city?

- What if I can never leave?

- What if I can never see my child again?

- Will my decision affect my kid's future and our relationship?

- Will I ever find someone who loves me?

- Can I ever trust someone else?

This is just the tip of the iceberg. There are thousands of such thoughts that rush through the mind of a victim when they decide to leave their abuser. Talking to a friend, family, or a counselor during such times can bring some light and make the burden a little easier to carry.

Recognizing the Warning Signs

The first and most indispensable step of leaving an abusive relationship is to identify the signs of abuse early. Trauma specialists believe that if victims can recognize the symptoms of physical or emotional violence during the early stages of the relationship, managing the damage becomes much more comfortable. It is also true that identifying the signs is harder than it sounds. Being in a close relationship often blurs our vision and subdues our judgment due to our emotions.

Some of the early signs of an abusive relationship include:

- Avoiding intimacy with the partner.

- Having little or no say in sex life.

- Forced intercourse.

- Partner always blaming you over little things.

- Partner spying on you and checking your phone

regularly.

- Public humiliation and being asked for explanations for everything.

- Being intentionally unapologetic even when it was the other person's fault.

- Irrational doubts about you seeing someone else or cheating on the partner. You may find it hard to make him/her trust you.

- Expressions of dissatisfaction about your financial status, or publicly insulting you for not having enough money.

- Frequent anger outbursts that may be triggered by alcohol or other substance consumptions.

- Bad mouthing about you in front of your kids.

- Insulting your family and not allowing you to contact or meet them.

- Displeasure about you working and spending more time with others.

If more than five of the above statements hold for you, it could mean that you are in an abusive relationship.

Creating a Safety Plan

Leaving the abuser is challenging when the victim is

in the same house. However, once the victim identifies the signs of abuse and recognizes the potential risks of staying with the abuser, he/she can create a safety nest around himself/herself.

Safety plans work while we are still around the abuser, and includes the following –

- Making a list of all emergency contacts on the phone, including friends, family, the ambulance, and the police.

- Having access to a phone at all times. If necessary, victims may keep an extra cell phone in case the victim seizes the other one.

- Using code words to communicate with friends and family about the torture. The abuser should not realize that the victim is seeking help.

- Writing down instances of or, if possible, recording the violent attacks for future evidence.

- Talking about the abuse soon after it has occurred. Delaying the process will make it more difficult for others to trust the victim.

- Always keeping child support services informed in case there is a child involved in the abuse.

- Having an emergency kit ready in case the victims have to leave under extreme threat.

Emergency Packing List For Victims of Domestic Violence and Relationship Abuse

Your safety should be your priority. Even though most victims feel they would never need to leave the house and that they can successfully handle the batterers at home, in most cases, it doesn't turn out that way.

Keep the following items ready and accessible. In a situation where you have to leave the house under severe threat, make sure you have all the items in the checklist below -

- Identity proofs and passports.
- Health insurance and visa (if you are staying overseas with the abuser).
- Financial papers, including bank details and credit cards.
- An extra set of mobile adapters.
- An extra copy of property papers or lease/rental records.
- Proof of marriage if the abuser is your spouse.
- Your car papers and keys.
- Any journal or recorder where you have noted down or recorded the abusive attacks.
- Some cash.
- A notebook with all the emergency contacts and addresses written.
- Clothes and other essentials.

If a child is involved in the abuse or is a part of the

family, then it is ideal to have his documents and other thingshandy as well

5 Things To Remember Before Making An Escape Plan

Most victims of domestic abuse go through emotional turmoil and are in two minds before deciding to do so. Some facts to consider before you go ahead with your decision are -

- Set realistic expectations

We all hope that things change magically, but they never do. Expecting the abuser to change or hoping that this is the last time it happens will keep the abuse going. Studies have shown that most abusers continue to misbehave with the victim because they feel that the victims are helpless and need the abusers' support to sustain. The only thing that victims should believe in is that they are self-dependent and are doing the right thing by standing up against the torture.

- Know that you cannot help the mistreater

Being on drugs or being temporarily intoxicated does not justify the abuser's behavior. Treating someone else with violence is a heinous act regardless of circumstance. It is natural for victims to try to help the abuser if they are in a close relationship, but in most instances, they make it worse for themselves. It is better to accept that you are living with an abuser, seek professional or legal help if you can, and move on before it is too late.

- Promises are meant to be broken.

There may be hundreds of promises that the mistreater makes each time after he commits a mistake. They may plead for a last chance, cry for help, play the victim, or hurt themselves to prove their love. In any case, victims should keep a firm grip on their rational thinking and be able to differentiate between the possible and impossible. Fake promises and pathological lying habits are traits that many abusers have in common.

- Don't worry about what happens after you leave.

"Will he be able to manage his food without me?" "Who will pack his bags when I am not around?" "Can our kids cope with the stress of their parents separating?"

Unfortunately, the scenario worsens when there is a child involved in the abuse. It is okay for victims to worry about the aftermath of their decision, but at the same time, ensuring safety for themselves and their kids are also equally important.

- You are not needy

If you talk to your friends about your situation or ask for help from your family, it does not mean that you are emotionally weak. Self-expression is a personal strength that helps victims of violence to move on and start again. It is common for abusers to make you feel vulnerable, but it is for you to continue believing in yourself and progress with confidence. Remember that it is okay to make mistakes or ask for help; being harsh on yourself is not on the cards at any point.

The Precursors To Leaving An Abusive Relationship

- Be prepared to leave at any moment.

If you have been in an abusive relationship for over one year, then there are chances that the violence will go on increasing with time. Be mentally prepared to leave the house at any point you feel your life is in danger. Keep your car fueledat all times and have the keys close to you so that you can grab them in case of an emergency. Keep the emergency bag as detailed above ready.

- Practice escaping

Practicing your escape can prevent victims from getting confused at the heat of the moment. Rehearse in your mind about how you can escape when the fight gets ugly or who to call if you are hurt. If you have kids, plan and rehearse for their escape as well.

- Have a backup plan

Escaping from an abuser who is close to us can be

tricky since he is already aware of our whereabouts and contacts. Keep a secret confidante, for example, a colleague that the abuser may not know, a relative, a neighbor, or an old friend. Inform them about your situation and let them know where you might seek refuge if you must leave the house in a panic.

- Do not compromise

If you have decided to leave the mistreater and choose a peaceful life for yourself, there is no probably little reason to rethink about it. Being self-compassionate is an essential requisite to heal your wounds. The perpetrator may invariably try to make you feel that it's your fault and portray themselves as the victims. Before excusing any ill-treatment, remember that –

- Verbal and emotional abuse are as unacceptable as physical violence.

- There may be worse forms of abuse you have heard of, but your experience still counts.

- Any act of abuse, no matter how small, is a sign that more such incidents can occur.

- If your submitting or tolerating the abuse helped in resolving the issue once, it does not mean that it will happen the same way again.

- **Keep the authorities informed**

As we saw earlier, a crucial aspect of the safety plan

is to have a reliable support system. Thankfully, there is a robust legal team supporting men and women of all ages facing abuse at home or outside. If you feel unsafe being around a person, no matter how close he/she is to you, inform the police or a community support worker about it.

Also, if you choose to stay with the abuser, you must contact a local violence support organization for emergency refuge. Choosing to move on from an abusive relationship is only one way of saving yourself. The burden of humiliation and assault remain and may keep hurting you unless you step forward and resolve it.

Even after leaving an abusive relationship, the mistreater may continue stalking the victim, sending messages, calling at vulnerable times of the day, or showing up everywhere they go. It is extremely important for victims to have a firm grip of themselves under such circumstances and, if possible, stay in a group to ensure safety.

Seeking professional assistance to overcome the trauma is entirely acceptable and often necessary to help victims move on with their lives. Individual therapy, group counseling, peer mental health programs, trauma interventions, and resilience training are some ways you could train yourself to recover from emotional distress.

Getting Out Of A Violent Relationship - Tips and Tricks

"It is still violence if the batterer does not hit you, choke you, or slam your head into a wall. If they degrade you, humiliate you, blame you, yell at you, lie to you, cheat on you, try to withhold your money, and attempt to control your life - it still counts as serious abuse."

In a toxic relationship like the ones we have discussed before, the victims often lose their identity and sense of self. If the victim is a child or a young adult, they might grow up to become indecisive, underconfident, and always look for someone to control their lives. Studies have shown that children who have been abused in their early years are more likely to get involved in abusive relationships in the future as well.

The control and dominance that accompanies a violent relationship take a toll on the victim's mental health, ultimately making him apathetic and doubtful about themselves. Some trauma specialists believe that 'even if it is not physical aggression, attempts at manipulating someone psychologically can lead to major depression, and in extreme cases, suicide."

Leaving a toxic relationship with a broken heart and an anxious mind is not easy. It takes a lot of courage and self-motivation to take a step forward and say 'no' to someone close to you. Finding the strength to walk out takes time and support, and here are some self-help strategies for victims that can help them execute their plan efficaciously.

- Reflect on yourself

Know yourself before you plan to move out. Studies have proved that abusers have a strong understanding of the victim's mind. He is aware of how the victims think and uses the knowledge to manipulate them emotionally.

The root of feeling trapped may lie inside the victim. So, before you move out, spend some time knowing your mind. Talk to a therapist, write thought journals, have a chat with your friends, practice mindfulness, and have a moment with yourself as often as you can. The clearer you get about your thought patterns and emotional experiences, the easier it will be to live an independent life successfully.

- Be sure if you want to give it another try

It may sound contradictory, but the fact is most victims who are abused by someone close try to find a reason to stay behind. The famous American psychologist and author Sherrie Bourg Carter suggested the following simple questions that victims of domestic violence can ask themselves to gain clarity of thoughts -

1. Do you like spending time with the abuser?

2. After spending some time together, do you feel your self-esteem has gone up or gone down?

3. When you are around the abuser, do you feel

emotionally and physically safe?

4. Do you think the abuser is right when he criticizes you or points at your mistakes?

5. When the abuser asks for an apology, do you believe that he is telling the truth?

Carter mentioned that if most of the answers to these questions are 'no,' it implies that the victim has lost trust and wants to move on with their lives. Having some vague answers may mean that you are still unsure whether this is abuse andyou may need external support to gain clarity.

Emotional Distancing

Abuse coming from families is the hardest one to get rid of. Nine times out of ten, families are imposed on us; we have no control, and neither do we have the choice to select who we are related to. More than 60% of incidents of sexual abuse in childhood are caused by people the children know and are close to - including family members, relatives, schoolteachers and other staff, servants, and the list goes on.

Abusers, in all forms, are *'emotional vampires'*. They establish their authority and suck away all the positive energy. The emotional blundering associated with any misbehavior makes the burden heavier to carry. A good idea to avoid this is emotionally distancing yourself from the abuser. Besides saving victims from being manipulated, emotionally distancing yourself also makes it easy to plan a life without the abuser dominating it. Some tips for detaching from the abuser include -

1. Not including them in your life decisions, such as changing jobs or buying a new car.

2. Managing your finances yourself.

3. Not sharing your day with the abuser.

4. Reducing communication to avoid conflicts.

5. Not spending time alone with the abuser.

6. Reducing physical intimacy (if the abuser is the spouse or partner).

7. Attending social gatherings without them.

8. Not participating in any decision that involves the abuser or his family.

- Self-determination

"You are so much stronger than your doubts… and more capable of pushing through the challenges that come your way." -T. Howard

Many abusive relationships are built on power games. If the batterer feels powerful and in charge of the victim's life, he feels emotionally satisfied and secure. Psychologists agree that showing confidence, even if you don't necessarily feel that confidence, can help in getting your autonomy back.

Simple answers like 'I can't' or 'I don't want to' can convey the right message to the abuser when he tries to get victims to do things they dislike. The victims can try to guard their emotional fragility and show self-determination in the following ways:

1. Saying 'no' without worrying about the consequences.

2. Sticking to their word no matter how hard the abuser tries to change it.

3. Not waiting for the abuser's approval for doing something.

4. Practicing positive self-affirmations such as 'I am trying my best', 'I know I can pull this off,' 'I am talented and capable of taking care of myself,' etc.

5. Complementing themselves and taking pride in their achievements.

6. Faking confidence to make sure the abuser thinks twice before being intimidating.

- Find support

It is natural for victims to feel weak and less empowered. We cannot emphasize enough how vital external support can be for getting rid of a problematic relationship. At any point, if the victims feel that they are unable to handle the situation themselves, they must find support and reach out for help. Support for domestic and relationship violence can come in the form of:

1. Friends, family, and coworkers.

2. Neighbors.

3. Social workers and community support.

4. Non-profit organizations that work for abuse victims.

5. Psychologists, counselors, or therapists.

6. Police, lawyers, or doctors.

As a responder to domestic violence or physical abuse, here are some points that we should always keep in mind :

- We must listen patiently to what the victims are trying to tell us.

- We should believe their words without being judgmental.

- We should comfort them and offer our support.

- We must encourage them to talk to a professional who can help.

- We should allow them to seek refuge in case of an emergency.

- If there are visible marks on the body, we must advise them to inform the police.

- If the victim is a child, we must help him/her get

to the right person and provide useful contact details (e.g., doctors, police, shelter homes, etc.).

Violence in any form is unacceptable irrespective of the abuser's age, sex, gender, or physical condition. However, when the abuser is someone we love or a part of our daily lives, letting go of the relationship seems complicated. Victims may unconsciously refuse to see the dark side of the person and choose to stay back despite the damage done to them.

Identifying the signs of abuse can help in early prevention and save the relationship from ending. If victims remember to respond early and build a secure support system, managing an abusive relationship becomes less stressful. We must not forget that a healthy relationship needs more than love to sustain. Unless there is mutual respect and freedom of expression, we cannot call it a successful interpersonal bond. Staying back may appease the abuser temporarily, but it ultimately damages the mental health of both the abuser and the victim.

You have decided not to tolerate the abuse anymore. You are now determined to start anew and be safe. You know that you deserve better, you know that you deserve to be happy and this what you will be seeking from now on. You feel more positive, more empowered, more self-motivated, and more confident. You feel ready to take a step forward in life. And you are now ready to clean up the mess that someone else created in your life.

Healing from abuse takes time. To quote Rebecca

Adamson, "It takes four generations to recover from every act of violence." Recovering from a traumatic relationship and starting a new life from there is never easy. It does not follow a linear path and is always different for everyone. When a victim tries to overcome the abuse and reconstruct his/her life from scratch, he/she is trying to overcome the injury frommonths and years of abuse. The process is never easy and takes a lot of struggle to reach the final point.

Moving out of an abusive relationship happens at four levels:

- Creating a safety plan.

- Building a secure escape plan.

- Executing the escape plan and leaving the abusive relationship behind.

- Rebuilding yourself and starting a new life.

We have seen the pre-planning stage and the strategies victims can follow to take themselves out of the violent environment successfully. In this part of the book, we will have a look at what happens after escaping from a troublesome relationship, and what it takes for victims to start all over again.

The longer the journey with trauma and abuse is, the more difficult the escape and recovery becomes. The aftereffects of emotional abuse are difficult to forget and heal from. The first and foremost 'mantra' to healing yourself after the damage is to give yourself as much time as you need. Everybody has their journey and their struggles; while some victims find it easier to move on in life, others may take years to get over the distress. Either way is excellent as long we keep trying and continue being self-compassionate.

The Freudian Interpretation

Before we move on to discussing how to rebuild yourself after the trauma, let us take a quick dive into the psychoanalytic interpretation of maintaining an abusive relationship. Sigmund Freud and his contemporary psychoanalysts carefully studied the underlying psychodynamics of why victims choose to stay in an abusive relationship in the first place. Their studies revealed that most women who had been in a violent relationship for more than five years found it difficult to leave the abuser despite all the sufferings and insults.

Freud called this phenomenon the 'compulsion to repeat.' He said that repeated exposure to trauma and abuse creates a cognitive distortion in the victims' minds and conditions, allowing them to justify the violent episodes. Also, Freud noted, victims who had early childhood experiences with trauma developed an unhealthy affinity of seeking the same. Their pleasure impulses remain consistent with what they have been experiencing in their childhood, even if it is entirely detrimental to them.

Although Freud's explanation faced intense

criticism, and most mental health professionals did not agree with his concept of 'self-destruction,' his research is still a strong base for psychoanalytic therapy in different settings.

Can Abusers Change?

The National Domestic Violence Hotline mentioned that only a handful of abusers could change themselves over time. Andthe few who could successfully become a better version of themselves underwent counseling and therapy to achieve that.

Changing the way they think can be challenging for abusers, especially when their victims are silent and unresponsive about the torture. Victims who decide to give their relationship another chance or contemplate about staying in an abusive relationship need to consider the possibility of the perpetrator changing or mending his ways. Asking the following questions to the mistreater can be an excellent start to evaluating his chances of improving.

Domestic Violence victims can encourage their partners to rate their responses on a 3-point scale, where '1' implies 'No,' '2' indicates 'Neutral,' and '3' means 'Yes.' More 'Yes' responses would suggest a greater possibility of the abuser improving himself.

Questions for the abuser	1 (No)	2 (Neutral)	3 (Yes)
1. Do you think you can express your anger without hurting me (the victim) or anyone else? 2. Do you believe you can talk without yelling or cursing when angry? 3. Do you think there is something inside you that needs to be changed? 4. Do you think it is okay for your partner to spend time doing things he/she likes to do? 5. Do you think you are ready to seek professional assistance for your behavior?			
Questions for the victims	**1 (No)**	**2 (Neutral)**	**3 (Yes)**
1. Do you think you will be safe around the abuser in the future? 2. Do you think your child is safe being around the batterer? 3. Do you feel it is okay to openly discuss your problems with the abuser?			

4.　　　Do you think you can trust the abuser fully? 5.　　　Do you think the abuser can repeat the same behavior with someone else once you have moved out? 6.　　　If your partner calls you or sends messages, would you want to respond to them voluntarily?			

Unless most of the answers are 'yes' to the above questions, we cannot say that there is a chance of the abuser changing.

Rebuilding Yourself After The Trauma

The scars of an abusive relationship can stay for a lifetime. According to Andrea Matthews, a famous mental health writer and professional, emotionally abusive relationships that involve curse words, shaming, and humiliation are worse than other forms of abuse. The damage done in such cases are rarely apparent but are strong enough to rip apart the victim's self-worth and sense of identity.

Most abusers attempt to take control of the victims' minds by statements such as -

- "Only I can care for you and love you the way you want."

- "You should choose between your family/friends

and me."

- "I never said that. And if I did, you made me say it."

- "You can never leave me. If you do, I will end my life."

- "You should dress up the way I want you to. I don't want others looking at you."

- "Why do we need to call friends over? We should enjoy ourselves."

- "Your work will drive you away from me."

- "You should allow me to handle your expenses."

If you have decided to put an end to the abusive relationship and build a better life for yourself, consider the following points to make the right move.

- Give yourself some time

"When I started to imagine my life without my partner, I was scared at first. But when I thought about it more, I realized that there would be no longer be anyone around to remind me that I am wrong every time I do something. I could decide things for myself and live my life as I have always wanted to."

Time has a vital role to play in moving on after an abusive relationship. Time has the power to heal the wounds and instill new hope. Although it doesn't take away the pain all at once, itrestores the self-confidence that the mistreater had ripped apart.

If you are starting a new life in a new place and want to leave behind all the painful memories of the torture you have faced, try spending more time with yourself, doing things that you love to do. You can start with the following:

1. Stay busy for as much as you can. It will divert your mind from the pain for the time being and help you get back on your feet quicker.

2. Spend some me-time as often as you want to. Go for a walk, book an appointment with your therapist, hop in for a massage or spa, read your favorite novel, or treat yourself with your favorite food. Put any effort that would make you feel special again.

3. Initially, you may find it challenging to manage on your own, especially if the mistreater had been your partner or if you were financially dependent on him/her. Try to get some support from family and friends to get through this rough patch. Remember that it is okay to feel weak and low, but do not move back in with your abuser without discussing it with your confidantes.

4. Get back to work as soon as you can. Getting the finances sorted can come as a huge relief when you are trying to live by yourself.

Take as much time as you need to recover from the

injury - physical, emotional, or both. An abusive relationship can tear your abilities apart for a while, but with the right support and self-belief, you can always get back to a healthy and normal functioning life.

- You come first

Being in an abusive relationship for years can make victims overlook their importance and ignore their needs and desires. When you are finally out of the batterer's grip, do all those things on your bucket list. Do everything that you always wanted to do and use your time whichever way you want to. Enjoy autonomy as much as you can, because you deserve it.

- Reestablish boundaries before letting someone into your life again

Limitations are essential when you decide to start over after a bad relationship. Many studies have shown that people who separate themselves from an abusive partner fear getting involved in close relationships later.

Establishing firm boundaries from day one is a great idea when you are trying to resettle. Healthy boundaries about handling one's own finances, being able to make personal decisions, and complete disagreement regarding physical violence can go a long way in sustaining the relationship for the long-term.

The most important thing to remember while drawing the line is to put yourself first. Come what may, it is never okay to tolerate insult and abuse from anyone you know.

- Clarify the truth

Victims of domestic violence or any type of relationship abuse often hear false rumors about them, many of which can come from the abuser himself. For example, many alcoholic and abusive men blame their partners for being the reason they resort to drugs. They can spread the word either to keep their image clean or to tarnish their partners' reputation in front of others.

For the first responders to domestic violence, this may be a tricky situation to judge.

Clarify all the false statements that you hear. If possible, make the abuser confess his lies, or as a victim, you can step up to have a one-on-one conversation with your close ones to make sure they don't have any misconceptions about you. Start your new life with no unwelcome burden of the past whatsoever.

Self-Help Assessment For Domestic Violence Victims

If you are still in two minds about whether you are in an abusive relationship or not, this assessment can help you come to a solution. It is a simple and straightforward assessment with practical questions about your day-to-day life. Respond 'yes' or 'no' to each statement. More 'yes' responses would indicate that you are living with a domestic abuser at home.

Instructions - Read the following statements and answer what you think is true to you. There are no right or wrong answers in this assessment. Take your time to complete it and evaluate your scores to identify whether you are living with an abusive partner or not.	Yes	No
1. My partner hurls curse words at me in public and privately.		
2. He/she humiliates me for my appearance, money, and family frequently.		
3. My partner does not allow me to be with my kids.		
4. I find it hard to express my opinions to my partner fearing he/she might disapprove and hurt me.		
5. I cannot predict my partner's mood and behavior.		
6. My partner threatens to kill me or hurt my child when I speak against him/her.		
7. My partner yells at me if I am late from work.		
8. My partner is doubtful about my fidelity and interrogates me every time I leave home.		
9. My partner forces me to be physically intimate even when I disagree.		
10. My partner decides my clothes, hair, and makeup.		

11. I find my partner irresponsible of his/her household duties and chores.		
12. He/she makes me feel unworthy and little.		
13. I feel I have been socially isolated after I moved in with my partner.		
14. My partner is unapologetic about hurting me physically.		
15. My partner is vocal about our intimate moments to others even after knowing it makes me uncomfortable.		
16. My partner controls every aspect of my life.		
17. I feel scared and suffocated when I am around him/her.		
18. I feel that my child is not safe with my partner around.		
19. My partner accuses me of provoking him/her to become violent.		
20. I often have to lie to my partner to avoid getting abused or beaten up.		

Intensive self-care strategies for victims of relationship and domestic violence

Self-care is vital for any victim who plans to or has started a new life after the trauma. Simple rejuvenating daily practices can help you overcome the stress and sew each thread of your new life with more control and resilience. Self-care regimes can vary from person to person. You should choose only those activities which give you the greatest pleasure and builds awareness in yourself. Here are some smooth and refreshing self-awareness tasks that you can treat yourself with.

- Listen to your body

Being kind to your body, for example, eating well, sleeping for at least 8 hours a day, and exercising regularly can help in fighting the grief that accompanies the painful separation of leaving an abuser. Moreover, in an abusive relationship, the victim often becomes alienated from his/her physical well-being. They are so engrossed in living up to their partners' expectations that self-love and self-care become a tertiary concern.

As a victim, you may have no choice over what you eat, when you have sex, or who you can be in touch with. But when you move out, you can regain control. Some useful tips for taking care of your body after leaving the abuser are:

1. Eat nutritious foods such as fresh fruits and veggies.

2. Go for a walk or a run as often as you want.

3. Engage in physical activities such as dancing, aerobics, swimming, etc., or any other sports you enjoy.

4. Stretch your muscles every morning and night.

- Connect and communicate

Abusers intentionally separate victims from their

family, friends, and close ones. When you are starting a new life out of the trauma, try to connect with more people in your social circle. Be proactive in calling friends over or attending social gatherings or community functions.

Initially, the anxiety of facing others and answering unwanted questions may bother you. Give it some time and try to stay in a closed circle where you feel comfortable.

Staying socially connected will help in facing the upcoming life challenges. Besides, you will gain more social support that can facilitate your survival after leaving your abusive relationship. Here are a few tips for actively engaging in social networks –

1. Call your friends and family once or twice a week and have light conversations about each other's lives.

2. Spend some time with friends during the weekends.

3. Attend family functions and work get-togethers.

4. Show up for coffee catch-ups.

5. Spend some quality time with your kids.

* Get organized

Arranging your time and physical space can help your mind and your thoughts get sorted. As you organize your room and your workspace, everything will seem to fall in place, and you will feel 'normal' again. Simple tweaks in daily life, such as storing your belongings in separate boxes instead of plastic bags, scheduling the day ahead every morning, or decluttering your room regularly are good ideas to start an organized lifestyle. The more organized you become, the more positivity you let into your life.

- Express your creative self

Self-expression is powerful. It helps in unwinding yourself and provides a secure space to express your emotions. Many victims of domestic violence and abuse find it extremely difficult to share their feelings or let others know how they feel. Engaging in creative activities can ease the process of self-expression and emotional catharsis. Choose any craft or art that you have always admired and spend some time doing that.

For example, studies have shown that drawing and related craft activities facilitate posttraumatic growth in children and adolescents. They find helps them express their emotions and find it to be a good way to adjust to the different circumstances of life.

- Be Grateful

The power of gratitude and appreciation overpowers everything else when it comes to self-healing. Simple gratitude meditations for 1-2 minutes every day can go a long way in creating a positive mindset and building a firm resilience inside you. You have struggled through the storm and have successfully overcome it. Take a moment to savor what is there with you now and acknowledge the beauty of a new beginning. As Buddha said, *"We become what we think."*

Conclusion

A s they say, "The hardest part lies ahead of you. There will still be trials and explanations, but they are easier to get through when you don't have to worry about your safety." It is natural for victims of violence to be afraid or regret their previous choices. Moving out and looking ahead in life after losing so much is a humongous job that can take years to internalize fully.

Abusers choose to inflict pain on us, but whether we allow the torture to take over our happiness and autonomy or not depends solely on us. With the tips and tricks mentioned in this book and valuable insights into the early signs of an abusive relationship, I hope you would find it easier to make the right decision at the right time. As a sufferer of abuse, you must remember to put your safety before anything else. As a first responder to violence, you should also not forget to trust believe a victim when they try to share their pain with you. Living a fulfilling life after a violent encounter may not be easy, but it is achievable with the right support.

www.ingramcontent.com/pod-product-compliance
Lightning Source LLC
Chambersburg PA
CBHW061351250726

48657CB00004B/1434